THE EXPANSION OF EUROPE THE CULMINATION OF MODERN HISTORY

By

RAMSAY MUIR

The Expansion of Europe The Culmination of Modern History

By **Ramsay Muir**

Copyright © 2023

ISBN: 978-93-58010-41-1

Published by

DOUBLE 9 BOOKS
2/13-B, Ansari Road, Daryaganj
New Delhi – 110002
info@double9books.com
www.double9books.com
Tel. 011-40042856

This book is under public domain

ABOUT THE AUTHOR

British historian, author, and lecturer Ramsay Muir (1872–1941) made major contributions to the study of European history. Muir was born in Otterburn, Northumberland, and attended the University College, Liverpool before going on to Balliol College in Oxford. Muir started teaching history as an assistant professor at the University of Manchester in 1898, and the following year he was hired as a lecturer at Liverpool. Muir was well-known for his engaging and approachable teaching methods and served as an instructor at a number of institutions in England, including the Universities of Manchester and Liverpool. The Growth of Europe: The Culmination of Modern History is still one of his most widely read books. He also wrote several books on European history. Muir was active in politics in addition to his academic career and represented the Scottish National Party in parliament from 1929 to 1931. From 1922 and 1935, Muir stood eight times for Parliament as a member of the Liberal Party. He was elected as the MP for Rochdale in Lancashire in the general election of 1923, but he lost that seat in 1924. The study of European history continues to be influenced by Muir's writing, and he is recognized as a gifted author and lecturer who made a substantial addition to our comprehension of the contemporary world.

CONTENTS

PREFACE 7

I — THE MEANING AND THE MOTIVES OF IMPERIALISM...............................9

II — THE ERA OF IBERIAN MONOPOLY 15

III — THE RIVALRY OF THE DUTCH, THE FRENCH AND
        THE ENGLISH, 1588-1763 21

IV — THE ERA OF REVOLUTION, 1763-1825 36

V — EUROPE AND THE NON-EUROPEAN WORLD 1815-1878 48

VI — THE TRANSFORMATION OF THE BRITISH EMPIRE, 1815-1878.............61

VII — THE ERA OF THE WORLD-STATES, 1878-1900 80

VIII — THE BRITISH EMPIRE AMID THE WORLD-POWERS, 1878-1914 109

IX — THE GREAT CHALLENGE, 1900-1914................................126

X — WHAT OF THE NIGHT? 144

PREFACE

The purpose of this book is twofold.

We realise to-day, as never before, that the fortunes of the world, and of every individual in it, are deeply affected by the problems of world-politics and by the imperial expansion and the imperial rivalries of the greater states of Western civilisation. But when men who have given no special attention to the history of these questions try to form a sound judgment on them, they find themselves handicapped by the lack of any brief and clear resume of the subject. I have tried, in this book, to provide such a summary, in the form of a broad survey, unencumbered with detail, but becoming fuller as it comes nearer to our own time. That is my first purpose. In fulfilling it I have had to cover much well-trodden ground. But I hope I have avoided the aridity of a mere compendium of facts.

My second purpose is rather more ambitious. In the course of my narrative I have tried to deal with ideas rather than with mere facts. I have tried to bring out the political ideas which are implicit in, or which result from, the conquest of the world by Western civilisation; and to show how the ideas of the West have affected the outer world, how far they have been modified to meet its needs, and how they have developed in the process. In particular I have endeavoured to direct attention to the significant new political form which we have seen coming into existence, and of which the British Empire is the oldest and the most highly developed example — the world-state, embracing peoples of many different types, with a Western nation-state as its nucleus. The study of this new form seems to me to be a neglected branch of political science, and one of vital importance. Whether or not it is to be a lasting form, time alone will show. Finally I have tried to display, in this long imperialist conflict, the strife of two rival conceptions of empire: the old, sterile, and ugly conception which thinks of empire as mere domination, ruthlessly pursued for the sole advantage of the master, and which seems to me to be most fully exemplified by Germany; and the nobler conception which regards empire as a trusteeship, and which is to be seen gradually emerging and struggling towards victory over the more brutal view, more clearly and in more varied forms in the story of the British Empire than in perhaps any other part of human history. That is why I have given a perhaps disproportionate attention to the British Empire. The war is determining, among other great issues, which of these conceptions is to dominate the future.

In its first form this book was completed in the autumn of 1916; and it contained, as I am bound to confess, some rather acidulated sentences in the passages which deal with the attitude of America towards European problems. These sentences were due to the deep disappointment which most Englishmen and most Frenchmen felt with the attitude of aloofness which America seemed to have adopted towards the greatest struggle for freedom and justice ever waged in history. It was an indescribable satisfaction to be forced by events to recognise that I was wrong, and that these passages of my book ought not to have been written as I wrote them. There is a sort of solemn joy in feeling that America, France, and Britain, the three nations which have contributed more than all the rest of the world put together to the establishment of liberty and justice on the earth, are now comrades in arms, fighting a supreme battle for these great causes. May this comradeship never be broken. May it bring about such a decision of the present conflict as will open a new era in the history of the world—a world now unified, as never before, by the final victory of Western civilisation which it is the purpose of this book to describe.

Besides rewriting and expanding the passages on America, I have seized the opportunity of this new issue to alter and enlarge certain other sections of the book, notably the chapter on the vital period 1878-1900, which was too slightly dealt with in the original edition. In this work, which has considerably increased the size of the book, I have been much assisted by the criticisms and suggestions of some of my reviewers, whom I wish to thank.

Perhaps I ought to add that though this book is complete in itself, it is also a sort of sequel to a little book entitled Nationalism and Internationalism, and was originally designed to be printed along with it: that is the explanation of sundry footnote references. The two volumes are to be followed by a third, on National Self-government, and it is my hope that the complete series may form a useful general survey of the development of the main political factors in modern history.

In its first form the book had the advantage of being read by my friend Major W. L. Grant, Professor of Colonial History at Queen's University Kingston, Ontario. The pressure of the military duties in which he is engaged has made it impossible for me to ask his aid in the revision of the book.

R. M. July 1917

I
THE MEANING AND THE MOTIVES OF IMPERIALISM

One of the most remarkable features of the modern age has been the extension of the influence of European civilisation over the whole world. This process has formed a very important element in the history of the last four centuries, and it has been strangely undervalued by most historians, whose attention has been too exclusively centred upon the domestic politics, diplomacies, and wars of Europe. It has been brought about by the creation of a succession of 'Empires' by the European nations, some of which have broken up, while others survive, but all of which have contributed their share to the general result; and for that reason the term 'Imperialism' is commonly employed to describe the spirit which has led to this astonishing and world-embracing movement of the modern age.

The terms 'Empire' and 'Imperialism' are in some respects unfortunate, because of the suggestion of purely military dominion which they convey; and their habitual employment has led to some unhappy results. It has led men of one school of thought to condemn and repudiate the whole movement, as an immoral product of brute force, regardless of the rights of conquered peoples. They have refused to study it, and have made no endeavour to understand it; not realising that the movement they were condemning was as inevitable and as irresistible as the movement of the tides—and as capable of being turned to beneficent ends. On the other hand, the implications of these terms have perhaps helped to foster in men of another type of mind an unhealthy spirit of pride in mere domination, as if that were an end in itself, and have led them to exult in the extension of national power, without closely enough considering the purposes for which it was to be used. Both attitudes are deplorable, and in so far as the words 'Empire,' 'Imperial,' and 'Imperialism' tend to encourage them, they are unfortunate words. They certainly do not adequately express the full significance of the process whereby the civilisation of Europe has been made into the civilisation of the world.

Nevertheless the words have to be used, because there are no others which at all cover the facts. And, after all, they are in some ways entirely appropriate. A great part of the world's area is inhabited by peoples who are still in a condition of barbarism, and seem to have rested in that condition for untold centuries. For such peoples the only chance of improvement was that they should pass under the dominion of more highly developed peoples; and to them a European 'Empire' brought, for the first time, not merely law and justice, but even the rudiments of the only kind of liberty which is worth having, the liberty which rests upon law. Another vast section of the world's population consists of peoples who have in some respects reached a high stage of civilisation, but who have failed to achieve for themselves a mode of organisation which could give them secure order and equal laws. For such peoples also the 'Empire' of Western civilisation, even when it is imposed and maintained by force, may bring advantages which will far outweigh its defects. In these cases the word 'Empire' can be used without violence to its original significance, and yet without apology; and these cases cover by far the greater part of the world.

The words 'Empire' and 'Imperialism' come to us from ancient Rome; and the analogy between the conquering and organising work of Rome and the empire-building work of the modern nation-states is a suggestive and stimulating analogy. The imperialism of Rome extended the modes of a single civilisation, and the Reign of Law which was its essence, over all the Mediterranean lands. The imperialism of the nations to which the torch of Rome has been handed on, has made the Reign of Law, and the modes of a single civilisation, the common possession of the whole world. Rome made the common life of Europe possible. The imperial expansion of the European nations has alone made possible the vision — nay, the certainty — of a future world-order. For these reasons we may rightly and without hesitation continue to employ these terms, provided that we remember always that the justification of any dominion imposed by a more advanced upon a backward or disorganised people is to be found, not in the extension of mere brute power, but in the enlargement and diffusion, under the shelter of power, of those vital elements in the life of Western civilisation which have been the secrets of its strength, and the greatest of its gifts to the world: the sovereignty of a just and rational system of law, liberty of person, of thought, and of speech, and, finally, where the conditions are favourable, the practice of self-government and the growth of that sentiment of common interest which we call the national spirit. These are the features of Western civilisation which have justified its conquest of the world[1]; and it must be for its success or failure in attaining these ends that we shall commend or condemn the imperial work of each of the nations which have shared in this vast achievement.

[1] See the first essay in Nationalism and Internationalism, in which an attempt is made to work out this idea.

Four main motives can be perceived at work in all the imperial activities of the European peoples during the last four centuries. The first, and perhaps the most potent, has been the spirit of national pride, seeking to express itself in the establishment of its dominion over less highly organised peoples. In the exultation which follows the achievement of national unity each of the nation-states in turn, if the circumstances were at all favourable, has been tempted to impose its power upon its neighbours,[2] or even to seek the mastery of the world. From these attempts have sprung the greatest of the European wars. From them also have arisen all the colonial empires of the European states. It is no mere coincidence that all the great colonising powers have been unified nation-states, and that their imperial activities have been most vigorous when the national sentiment was at its strongest among them. Spain, Portugal, England, France, Holland, Russia: these are the great imperial powers, and they are also the great nation-states. Denmark and Sweden have played a more modest part, in extra-European as in European affairs. Germany and Italy only began to conceive imperial ambitions after their tardy unification in the nineteenth century. Austria, which has never been a nation-state, never became a colonising power. Nationalism, then, with its eagerness for dominion, may be regarded as the chief source of imperialism; and if its effects are unhappy when it tries to express itself at the expense of peoples in whom the potentiality of nationhood exists, they are not necessarily unhappy in other cases. When it takes the form of the settlement of unpeopled lands, or the organisation and development of primitive barbaric peoples, or the reinvigoration and strengthening of old and decadent societies, it may prove itself a beneficent force. But it is beneficent only in so far as it leads to an enlargement of law and liberty.

[2] Nationalism and Imperialism.

The second of the blended motives of imperial expansion has been the desire for commercial profits; and this motive has played so prominent a part, especially in our own time, that we are apt to exaggerate its force, and to think of it as the sole motive. No doubt it has always been present in some degree in all imperial adventures. But until the nineteenth century it probably formed the predominant motive only in regard to the acquisition of tropical lands. So long as Europe continued to be able to produce as much as she needed of the food and the raw materials for industry that her soil and climate were capable of yielding, the commercial motive for acquiring territories in the temperate zone, which could produce only commodities of the same type, was comparatively weak; and the European settlements in these areas, which we have come to regard as the most important products of the imperialist movement, must in their origin and early settlement be mainly attributed to other than commercial motives. But Europe has always depended for most of her luxuries upon the tropics: gold and ivory and gems, spices and sugar and fine woven stuffs, from a very early age found their way into Europe from India and the East, coming by slow and devious caravan routes to the shores of the Black Sea and the Mediterranean. Until the end of the fifteenth century the European trader had no direct contact with the sources of these precious commodities; the supply of them was scanty and the price high. The desire to gain a more direct access to the sources of this traffic, and to obtain control of the supply, formed the principal motive for the great explorations. But these, in their turn, disclosed fresh tropical areas worth exploiting, and introduced new luxuries, such as tobacco and tea, which soon took rank as necessities. They also brought a colossal increment of wealth to the countries which had undertaken them. Hence the acquisition of a share in, or a monopoly of, these lucrative lines of trade became a primary object of ambition to all the great states. In the nineteenth century Europe began to be unable to supply her own needs in regard to the products of the temperate zone, and therefore to desire control over other areas of this type; but until then it was mainly in regard to the tropical or sub-tropical areas that the commercial motive formed the predominant element in the imperial rivalries of the nation-states. And even to-day it is over these areas that their conflicts are most acute.

A third motive for imperial expansion, which must not be overlooked, is the zeal for propaganda: the eagerness of virile peoples to propagate the religious and political ideas which they have adopted. But this is only another way of saying that nations are impelled upon the imperial career by the desire to extend the influence of their conception of civilisation, their Kultur. In one form or another this motive has always been present. At first it took the form of religious zeal. The spirit of the Crusaders was inherited by the Portuguese and the Spaniards, whose whole history had been one long crusade against the Moors. When the Portuguese started upon the exploration of the African coast, they could scarcely have sustained to the end that long and arduous task if they had been allured by no other prospect than the distant hope of finding a new route to the East. They were buoyed up also by the desire to strike a blow for Christianity. They expected to find the mythical Christian empire of Prester John, and to join hands with him in overthrowing the infidel. When Columbus persuaded Queen Isabella of Castile to supply the means for his madcap adventure, it was by a double inducement that he won her assent: she was to gain access to the wealth of the Indies, but she was also to be the means of converting the heathen to a knowledge of Christianity; and this double motive continually recurs in the early history of the Spanish Empire. France could scarcely, perhaps, have persisted in maintaining her far from profitable settlements on the barren shores of the St. Lawrence if the missionary motive had not existed alongside of the motives of national pride and the desire for profits: her great work of exploration in the region of the Great Lakes and the Mississippi Valley was due quite as much to the zeal of the heroic missionaries of the Jesuit and other orders as to the enterprise of trappers and traders. In English colonisation, indeed, the missionary motive was never, until the nineteenth century, so strongly marked. But its place was taken by a parallel political motive. The belief that they were diffusing the free institutions in which they took so much pride certainly formed an element in the colonial activities of the English. It is both foolish and unscientific to disregard this element of propaganda in the imperialist movement, still more to treat the assertion of it by the colonising powers as mere hypocrisy. The motives of imperial expansion, as of other human activities, are mixed, and the loftier elements in them are not often predominant. But the loftier elements are always present. It is hypocrisy to pretend that they are alone or even chiefly operative. But it is cynicism wholly to deny their influence. And of the two sins cynicism is the worse, because by over-emphasising it strengthens and cultivates the lower among the mixed motives by which men are ruled.

The fourth of the governing motives of imperial expansion is the need of finding new homes for the surplus population of the colonising people. This was not in any country a very powerful motive until the nineteenth century, for over-population did not exist in any serious degree in any of the European states until that age. Many of the political writers in seventeenth-century England, indeed, regarded the whole movement of colonisation with alarm, because it seemed to be drawing off men who could not be spared. But if the population was nowhere excessive, there were in all countries certain classes for which emigration to new lands offered a desired opportunity. There were the men bitten with the spirit of adventure, to whom the work of the pioneer presented an irresistible attraction. Such men are always numerous in virile communities, and when in any society their numbers begin to diminish, its decay is at hand. The imperial activities of the modern age have more than anything else kept the breed alive in all European countries, and above all in Britain. To this type belonged the conquistadores of Spain, the Elizabethan seamen, the French explorers of North America, the daring Dutch navigators. Again, there were the younger sons of good family for whom the homeland presented small opportunities, but who found in colonial settlements the chance of creating estates like those of their fathers at home, and carried out with them bands of followers drawn from among the sons of their fathers' tenantry. To this class belonged most of the planter-settlers of Virginia, the seigneurs of French Canada, the lords of the great Portuguese feudal holdings in Brazil, and the dominant class in all the Spanish colonies. Again, there were the 'undesirables' of whom the home government wanted to be rid—

convicts, paupers, political prisoners; they were drafted out in great numbers to the new lands, often as indentured servants, to endure servitude for a period of years and then to be merged in the colonial population. When the loss of the American colonies deprived Britain of her dumping-ground for convicts, she had to find a new region in which to dispose of them; and this led to the first settlement of Australia, six years after the establishment of American independence. Finally, in the age of bitter religious controversy there was a constant stream of religious exiles seeking new homes in which they could freely follow their own forms of worship. The Puritan settlers of New England are the outstanding example of this type. But they were only one group among many. Huguenots from France, Moravians from Austria, persecuted 'Palatines' and Salzburgers from Germany, poured forth in an almost unbroken stream. It was natural that they should take refuge in the only lands where full religious freedom was offered to them; and these were especially some of the British settlements in America, and the Dutch colony at the Cape of Good Hope.

It is often said that the overflow of Europe over the world has been a sort of renewal of the folk-wandering of primitive ages. That is a misleading view: the movement has been far more deliberate and organised, and far less due to the pressure of external circumstances, than the early movements of peoples in the Old World. Not until the nineteenth century, when the industrial transformation of Europe brought about a really acute pressure of population, can it be said that the mere pressure of need, and the shortage of sustenance in their older homes, has sent large bodies of settlers into the new lands. Until that period the imperial movement has been due to voluntary and purposive action in a far higher degree than any of the blind early wanderings of peoples. The will-to-dominion of virile nations exulting in their nationhood; the desire to obtain a more abundant supply of luxuries than had earlier been available, and to make profits therefrom; the zeal of peoples to impose their mode of civilisation upon as large a part of the world as possible; the existence in the Western world of many elements of restlessness and dissatisfaction, adventurers, portionless younger sons, or religious enthusiasts: these have been the main operative causes of this huge movement during the greater part of the four centuries over which it has extended. And as it has sprung from such diverse and conflicting causes, it has assumed an infinite variety of forms; and both deserves and demands a more respectful study as a whole than has generally been given to it.

II

THE ERA OF IBERIAN MONOPOLY

During the Middle Ages the contact of Europe with the rest of the world was but slight. It was shut off by the great barrier of the Islamic Empire, upon which the Crusades made no permanent impression; and although the goods of the East came by caravan to the Black Sea ports, to Constantinople, to the ports of Syria, and to Egypt, where they were picked up by the Italian traders, these traders had no direct knowledge of the countries which were the sources of their wealth. The threat of the Empire of Genghis Khan in the thirteenth century aroused the interest of Europe, and the bold friars, Carpini and Rubruquis, made their way to the centres of that barbaric sovereign's power in the remote East, and brought back stories of what they had seen; later the Poli, especially the great Marco, undertook still more daring and long-continued journeys, which made India and Cathay less unreal to Europeans, and stimulated the desire for further knowledge. The later mediaeval maps of the world, like that of Fra Mauro (1459),[3] which incorporate this knowledge, are less wildly imaginative than their predecessors, and show a vague notion of the general configuration of the main land-masses in the Old World. But beyond the fringes of the Mediterranean the world was still in the main unknown to, and unaffected by, European civilisation down to the middle of the fifteenth century.

[3] Simplified reproductions of this and the other early maps alluded to are printed in Philip's Students' Atlas of Modern History, which also contains a long series of maps illustrating the extra-Europeans activities of the European states.

Then, suddenly, came the great era of explorations, which were made possible by the improvements in navigation worked out during the fifteenth century, and which in two generations incredibly transformed the aspect of the world. The marvellous character of this revelation can perhaps be illustrated by the comparison of two maps, that of Behaim, published in 1492, and that of Schoener, published in 1523. Apart from its adoption of the theory that the earth was globular, not round and flat, Behaim's map shows little advance upon Fra Mauro, except that it gives a clearer idea of the shape of Africa, due to the earlier explorations of the Portuguese. But Schoener's map shows that the broad outlines of the distribution of the land-masses of both hemispheres were already in 1523 pretty clearly understood. This astonishing advance was due to the daring and enterprise of the Portuguese explorers, Diaz, Da Gama, Cabral, and of the adventurers in the service of Spain, Columbus, Balboa, Vespucci, and — greatest of them all — Magellan.

These astonishing discoveries placed for a time the destinies of the outer world in the hands of Spain and Portugal, and the first period of European imperialism is the period of Iberian monopoly, extending to 1588. A Papal award in 1493 confirmed the division of the non-European world between the two powers, by a judgment which the orthodox were bound to accept, and did accept for two generations. All the oceans, except the North Atlantic, were closed to the navigators of other nations; and these two peoples were given, for a century, the opportunity of showing in what guise they would introduce the civilisation of Europe to the rest of the globe. Pioneers as they were in the work of imperial development, it is not surprising that they should have made great blunders; and in the end their foreign dominions weakened rather than strengthened the home countries, and contributed to drag them down from the high place which they had taken among the nations.

The Portuguese power in the East was never more than a commercial dominion. Except in Goa, on the west coast of India, no considerable number of settlers established themselves at any point; and the Goanese settlement is the only instance of the formation of a mixed race, half Indian and half European. Wherever the Portuguese power was established, it proved itself hard and intolerant; for the spirit of the Crusader was ill-adapted to the establishment of good relations with the non-Christian peoples. The rivalry of Arab traders in the Indian Ocean was mercilessly destroyed, and there was as little mercy for the Italian merchants, who found the stream of goods that the Arabs had sent them by way of the Red Sea and the Persian Gulf almost wholly intercepted. No doubt any other people, finding itself in the position which the Portuguese occupied in the early sixteenth century, would have been tempted to use their power in the same way to establish a complete monopoly; but the success with which the Portuguese attained their aim was in the end disastrous to them. It was followed by, if it did not cause, a rapid deterioration of the ability with which their affairs were directed; and when other European traders began to appear in the field, they were readily welcomed by the princes of India and the chieftains of the Spice Islands. In the West the Portuguese settlement in Brazil was a genuine colony, or branch of the Portuguese nation, because here there existed no earlier civilised people to be dominated. But both in East and West the activities of the Portuguese were from the first subjected to an over-rigid control by the home government.

Eager to make the most of a great opportunity for the national advantage, the rulers of Portugal allowed no freedom to the enterprise of individuals. The result was that in Portugal itself, in the East, and in Brazil, initiative was destroyed, and the brilliant energy which this gallant little nation had displayed evaporated within a century. It was finally destroyed when, in 1580, Portugal and her empire fell under the dominion of Spain, and under all the reactionary influences of the government of Philip II. By the time this heavy yoke was shaken off, in the middle of the seventeenth century, the Portuguese dominion had fallen into decay. To-day nothing of it remains save 'spheres of influence' on the western and eastern coasts of Africa, two or three ports on the coast of India, the Azores, and the island of Magao off the coast of China.

The Spanish dominion in Central and South America was of a different character. When once they had realised that it was not a new route to Asia, but a new world, that Columbus had discovered for them, the Spaniards sought no longer mainly for the riches to be derived from traffic, but for the precious metals, which they unhappily discovered in slight quantities in Hispaniola, but in immense abundance in Mexico and Peru. It is impossible to exaggerate the heroic valour and daring of Cortez, Pizarro, Hernando de Soto, Orellana, and the rest of the conquistadores who carved out in a single generation the vast Spanish empire in Central and South America; but it is equally impossible to exaggerate their cruelty, which was born in part of the fact that they were a handful among myriads, in part of the fierce traditions of crusading warfare against the infidel. Yet without undervaluing their daring, it must be recognised that they had a comparatively easy task in conquering the peoples of these tropical lands. In the greater islands of the West Indies they found a gentle and yielding people, who rapidly died out under the forced labour of the mines and plantations, and had to be replaced by negro slave-labour imported from Africa. In Mexico and Peru they found civilisations which on the material side were developed to a comparatively high point, and which collapsed suddenly when their governments and capitals had been overthrown; while their peoples, habituated to slavery, readily submitted to a new servitude. It must be recognised, to the honour of the government of Charles V. and his successors, that they honestly attempted to safeguard the usages and possessions of the conquered peoples, and to protect them in some degree against the exploitation of their conquerors. But it was the protection of a subject race doomed to the condition of Helotage; they were protected, as the Jews were protected by the kings of mediaeval England, because they were a valuable asset of the crown. The policy of the Spanish government did not avail to prevent an intermixture of the races, because the Spaniards themselves came from a sub-tropical country, and the Mexicans and Peruvians especially were separated from them by no impassable gulf such as separates the negro or the Australian bushman from the white man. Central and Southern America thus came to be peopled by a hybrid race, speaking Spanish, large elements of which were conscious of their own inferiority. This in itself would perhaps have been a barrier to progress. But the concentration of attention upon the precious metals, and the neglect of industry due to this cause and to the employment of slave-labour, formed a further obstacle. And in addition to all, the Spanish government, partly with a view to the execution of its native policy, partly because it regarded the precious metals as the chief product of these lands and wished to maintain close control over them, and partly because centralised autocracy was carried to its highest pitch in Spain, allowed little freedom of action to the local governments, and almost none to the settlers. It treated the trade of these lands as a monopoly of the home country, to be carried on under the most rigid control. It did little or nothing to develop the natural resources of the empire, but rather discouraged them lest they should compete with the labours of the mine; and in what concerned the intellectual welfare of its subjects, it limited itself, as in Spain, to ensuring that no infection of heresy or freethought should reach any part of its dominions. All this had a deadening effect; and the surprising thing is, not that the Spanish Empire should have fallen into an early decrepitude, but that it should have shown such comparative vigour, tenacity, and power of expansion as it actually exhibited. Not until the nineteenth century did the vast natural resources of these regions begin to undergo any rapid development; that is to say, not until most of the settlements had discarded the connection with Spain; and even then, the defects bred into the people by three centuries of reactionary and unenlightened government produced in them an incapacity to use their newly won freedom, and condemned these lands to a long period of anarchy. It would be too strong to say that it would have been better had the Spaniards never come to America; for, when all is said, they have done more than any other people, save the British, to plant European modes of life in the non-European world. But it is undeniable that their dominion afforded a far from happy illustration of the working of Western civilisation in a new field, and exercised a very unfortunate reaction upon the life of the mother-country.

The conquest of Portugal and her empire by Philip II., in 1580, turned Spain into a Colossus bestriding the world, and it was inevitable that this world-dominion should be challenged by the other European states which faced upon the Atlantic. The challenge was taken up by three nations, the English, the French, and the Dutch, all the more readily because the very existence of all three and the religion of two of them were threatened by the apparently overwhelming strength of Spain in Europe. As in so many later instances, the European conflict was inevitably extended to the non-European world. From the middle of the sixteenth century onwards these three peoples attempted, with increasing daring, to circumvent or to undermine the Spanish power, and to invade the sources of the wealth which made it dangerous to them; but the attempt, so far as it was made on the seas and beyond them, was in the main, and for a long time, due to the spontaneous energies of volunteers, not to the action of governments. Francis I. of France sent out the Venetian Verazzano to explore the American shores of the North Atlantic, as Henry VII. of England had earlier sent the Genoese Cabots. But nothing came of these official enterprises. More effective were the pirate adventurers who preyed upon the commerce between Spain and her possessions in the Netherlands as it passed through the Narrow Seas, running the gauntlet of English, French, and Dutch. More effective still were the attempts to find new routes to the East, not barred by the Spanish dominions, by a north-east or a north-west passage; for some of the earlier of these adventures led to fruitful unintended consequences, as when the Englishman Chancellor, seeking for a north-east passage, found the route to Archangel and opened up a trade with Russia, or as when the Frenchman Cartier, seeking for a north-west passage, hit upon the great estuary of the St. Lawrence, and marked out a claim for France to the possession of the area which it drained. Most effective of all were the smuggling and piratical raids into the reserved waters of West Africa and the West Indies, and later into the innermost penetralia of the Pacific Ocean, which were undertaken with rapidly increasing boldness by the navigators of all three nations, but above all by the English. Drake is the supreme exponent of these methods; and his career illustrates in the clearest fashion the steady diminution of Spanish prestige under these attacks, and the growing boldness and maritime skill of its attackers.

From the time of Drake's voyage round the world (1577) and its insulting defiance of the Spanish power on the west coast of South America, it became plain that the maintenance of Spanish monopoly could not last much longer. It came to its end, finally and unmistakably, in the defeat of the Grand Armada. That supreme victory threw the ocean roads of trade open, not to the English only, but to the sailors of all nations. In its first great triumph the English navy had established the Freedom of the Seas, of which it has ever since been the chief defender. Since 1588 no power has dreamt of claiming the exclusive right of traversing any of the open seas of the world, as until that date Spain and Portugal had claimed the exclusive right of using the South Atlantic, the Pacific, and the Indian Oceans.

So ends the first period in the imperial expansion of the Western peoples, the period of Spanish and Portuguese monopoly. Meanwhile, unnoticed in the West, a remarkable eastward expansion was being effected by the Russian people. By insensible stages they had passed the unreal barrier between

Europe and Asia, and spread themselves thinly over the vast spaces of Siberia, subduing and assimilating the few and scattered tribes whom they met; by the end of the seventeenth century they had already reached the Pacific Ocean. It was a conquest marked by no great struggles or victories, an insensible permeation of half a continent. This process was made the easier for the Russians, because in their own stock were blended elements of the Mongol race which they found scattered over Siberia: they were only reversing the process which Genghis Khan had so easily accomplished in the thirteenth century. And as the Russians had scarcely yet begun to be affected by Western civilisation, there was no great cleavage or contrast between them and their new subjects, and the process of assimilation took place easily. But the settlement of Siberia was very gradual. At the beginning of the eighteenth century the total population of this vast area amounted to not more than 300,000 souls, and it was not until the nineteenth century that there was any rapid increase.

III

THE RIVALRY OF THE DUTCH, THE FRENCH AND THE ENGLISH, 1588-1763

The second period of European imperialism was filled with the rivalries of the three nations which had in different degrees contributed to the breakdown of the Spanish monopoly, the Dutch, the French, and the English; and we have next to inquire how far, and why, these peoples were more successful than the Spaniards in planting in the non-European world the essentials of European civilisation. The long era of their rivalry extended from 1588 to 1763, and it can be most conveniently divided into three sections. The first of these extended from 1588 to about 1660, and may be called the period of experiment and settlement; during its course the leadership fell to the Dutch. The second extended from 1660 to 1713, and may be called the period of systematic colonial policy, and of growing rivalry between France and England. The third, from 1713 to 1763, was dominated by the intense rivalry of these two countries, decadent Spain joining in the conflict on the side of France, while the declining power of the Dutch was on the whole ranged on the side of Britain; and it ended with the complete ascendancy of Britain, supreme at once in the West and in the East.

(a) The Period of Settlement, 1588-1660

The special interest of the first half of the seventeenth century is that in the trading and colonial experiments of this period the character of the work which was to be done by the three new candidates for extra-European empire was already very clearly and instructively displayed. They met as rivals in every field: in the archipelago of the West Indies, and the closely connected slaving establishments of West Africa, in the almost empty lands of North America, and in the trading enterprises of the far East; and everywhere a difference of spirit and method appeared.

The Dutch, who made a far more systematic and more immediately profitable use of the opportunity than either of their rivals, regarded the whole enterprise as a great national commercial venture. It was conducted by two powerful trading corporations, the Company of the East Indies and the Company of the West Indies; but though directed by the merchants of Amsterdam, these were genuinely national enterprises; their shareholders were drawn from every province and every class; and they were backed by all the influence which the States-General of the United Provinces – controlled during this period mainly by the commercial interest – was able to wield.

The Company of the East Indies was the richer and the more powerful of the two, because the trade of the Far East was beyond comparison the most lucrative in the world. Aiming straight at the source of the greatest profits – the trade in spices – the Dutch strove to establish a monopoly control over the Spice Islands and, in general, over the Malay Archipelago; and they were so successful that their influence remains to-day predominant in this region. Their first task was to overthrow the ascendancy of the Portuguese, and in this they were willing to co-operate with the English traders. But the bulk of the work was done by the Dutch, for the English East India Company was poor in comparison with the Dutch, was far less efficiently organised, and, in especial, could not count upon the steady support of the national government. It was mainly the Dutch who built forts and organised factories, because they alone had sufficient capital to maintain heavy standing charges. Not unnaturally they did not see why the English should reap any part of the advantage of their work, and set themselves to establish a monopoly. In the end the English were driven out with violence. After the Massacre of Amboyna (1623) their traders disappeared from these seas, and the Dutch supremacy remained unchallenged until the nineteenth century.

It was a quite intolerant commercial monopoly which they had instituted, but from the commercial point of view it was administered with great intelligence. Commercial control brought in its train territorial sovereignty, over Java and many of the neighbouring islands; and this sovereignty was exercised by the directors of the company primarily with a view to trade interests. It was a trade despotism, but a trade despotism wisely administered, which gave justice and order to its native subjects. On the mainland of India the Dutch never attained a comparable degree of power, because the native states were strong enough to hold them in check. But in this period their factories were more numerous and more prosperous than those of the English, their chief rivals; and over the island of Ceylon they established an ascendancy almost as complete as that which they had created in the archipelago.

They were intelligent enough also to see the importance of good calling-stations on the route to the East. For this purpose they planted a settlement in Mauritius, and another at the Cape of Good Hope. But these settlements were never regarded as colonies. They were stations belonging to a trading company; they remained under its complete control, and were allowed no freedom of development, still less any semblance of self-government. If Cape

Colony grew into a genuine colony, or offshoot of the mother-country, it was in spite of the company, not by reason of its encouragement, and from first to last the company's relations with the settlers were of the most unhappy kind. For the company would do nothing at the Cape that was not necessary for the Eastern trade, which was its supreme interest, and the colonists naturally did not take the same view. It was this concentration upon purely commercial aims which also prevented the Dutch from making any use of the superb field for European settlement opened up by the enterprise of their explorers in Australia and New Zealand. These fair lands were left unpeopled, largely because they promised no immediate trade profits.

In the West the enterprises of the Dutch were only less vigorous than in the East, and they were marked by the same feature of an intense concentration upon the purely commercial aspect. While the English and (still more) the French adventurers made use of the lesser West Indian islands, unoccupied by Spain, as bases for piratical attacks upon the Spanish trade, the Dutch, with a shrewd instinct, early deserted this purely destructive game for the more lucrative business of carrying on a smuggling trade with the Spanish mainland; and the islands which they acquired (such as Curayoa) were, unlike the French and English islands, especially well placed for this purpose. They established a sugar colony in Guiana. But their main venture in this region was the conquest of a large part of Northern Brazil from the Portuguese (1624); and here their exploitation was so merciless, under the direction of the Company of the West Indies, that the inhabitants, though they had been dissatisfied with the Portuguese government, and had at first welcomed the Dutch conquerors, soon revolted against them, and after twenty years drove them out.

On the mainland of North America the Dutch planted a single colony — the New Netherlands, with its capital at New Amsterdam, later New York. Their commercial instinct had once more guided them wisely. They had found the natural centre for the trade of North America; for by way of the river Hudson and its affluent, the Mohawk, New York commands the only clear path through the mountain belt which everywhere shuts off the Atlantic coast region from the central plain of America. Founded and controlled by the Company of the West Indies, this settlement was intended to be, not primarily the home of a branch of the Dutch nation beyond the seas, but a trading-station for collecting the furs and other products of the inland regions. At Orange (Albany), which stands at the junction of the Mohawk and the Hudson, the Dutch traders collected the furs brought in by Indian trappers from west and north; New Amsterdam was the port of export; and if settlers were encouraged, it was only that they might supply the men and the means and the food for carrying on this traffic. The Company of the West Indies administered the colony purely from this point of view. No powers of self-government were allowed to the settlers; and, as in Cape Colony, the relations between the colonists and the governing company were never satisfactory, because the colonists felt that their interests were wholly subordinated.

The distinguishing feature of French imperial activity during this period was its dependence upon the support and direction of the home government, which was the natural result of the highly centralised regime established in France during the modern era. Only in one direction was French activity successfully maintained by private enterprise, and this was in the not very reputable field of West Indian buccaneering, in which the French were even more active than their principal rivals and comrades, the English. The word 'buccaneer' itself comes from the French: boucan means the wood-fire at which the pirates dried and smoked their meat, and these fires, blazing on deserted islands, must often have warned merchant vessels to avoid an ever-present danger. The island of Tortuga, which commands the passage between Cuba and Hispaniola through which the bulk of the Spanish traffic passed on its way from Mexico to Europe, was the most important of the buccaneering bases, and although it was at first used by the buccaneers of all nations, it soon became a purely French possession, as did, later, the adjoining portion of the island of Hispaniola (San Domingo). The French did, indeed, like the English, plant sugar colonies in some of the lesser Antilles; but during the first half of the seventeenth century they attained no great prosperity.

For the greater enterprises of trade in the East and colonisation in the West, the French relied almost wholly upon government assistance, and although both Henry IV. in the first years of the century, and Richelieu in its second quarter, were anxious to give what help they could, internal dissensions were of such frequent occurrence in France during this period that no systematic or continuous governmental aid was available. Hence the French enterprises both in the East and in the West were on a small scale, and achieved little success. The French East India Company was all but extinct when Colbert took it in hand in 1664; it was never able to compete with its Dutch or even its English rival.

But the period saw the establishment of two French colonies in North America: Acadia (Nova Scotia) on the coast, and Canada, with Quebec as its centre, in the St. Lawrence valley, separated from one another on land by an almost impassable barrier of forest and mountain. These two colonies were founded, the first in 1605 and the second in 1608, almost at the same moment as the first English settlement on the American continent. They had a hard struggle during the first fifty years of their existence; for the number of settlers was very small, the soil was barren, the climate severe, and the Red

Indians, especially the ferocious Iroquois towards the south, were far more formidable enemies than those who bordered on the English colonies.

There is no part of the history of European colonisation more full of romance and of heroism than the early history of French Canada; an incomparable atmosphere of gallantry and devotion seems to overhang it. From the first, despite their small numbers and their difficulties, these settlers showed a daring in exploration which was only equalled by the Spaniards, and to which there is no parallel in the records of the English colonies. At the very outset the great explorer Champlain mapped out the greater part of the Great Lakes, and thus reached farther into the continent than any Englishman before the end of the eighteenth century; and although this is partly explained by the fact that the St. Lawrence and the lakes afforded an easy approach to the interior, while farther south the forest-clad ranges of the Alleghanies constituted a very serious barrier, this does not diminish the French pre-eminence in exploration. Nor can anything in the history of European colonisation surpass the heroism of the French missionaries among the Indians, who faced and endured incredible tortures in order to bring Christianity to the barbarians. No serious missionary enterprise was ever undertaken by the English colonists; this difference was in part due to the fact that the missionary aim was definitely encouraged by the home government in France. From the outset, then, poverty, paucity of numbers, gallantry, and missionary zeal formed marked features of the French North American colonies.

In other respects they very clearly reproduced some of the features of the motherland. Their organisation was strictly feudal in character. The real unit of settlement and government was the seigneurie, an estate owned by a Frenchman of birth, and cultivated by his vassals, who found refuge from an Indian raid, or other danger, in the stockaded house which took the place of a chateau, much as their remote ancestors had taken refuge from the raids of the Northmen in the castles of their seigneur's ancestors. And over this feudal society was set, as in France, a highly centralised government wielding despotic power, and in its turn absolutely subject to the mandate of the Crown at home. This despotic government had the right to require the services of all its subjects in case of need; and it was only the centralised government of the colony, and the warlike and adventurous character of its small feudalised society, which enabled it to hold its own for so long against the superior numbers but laxer organisation of its English neighbours. A despotic central power, a feudal organisation, and an entire dependence upon the will of the King of France and upon his support, form, therefore, the second group of characteristics which marked the French colonies. They were colonies in the strictest sense, all the more because they reproduced the main features of the home system.

Nothing could have differed more profoundly from this system than the methods which the English were contemporaneously applying, without plan or clearly defined aim, and guided only by immediate practical needs, and by the rooted traditions of a self-governing people. Their enterprises received from the home government little direct assistance, but they throve better without it; and if there was little assistance, there was also little interference. In the East the English East India Company had to yield to the Dutch the monopoly of the Malayan trade, and bitterly complained of the lack of government support; but it succeeded in establishing several modest factories on the coast of India, and was on the whole prosperous. But it was in the West that the distinctive work of the English was achieved during this period, by the establishment of a series of colonies unlike any other European settlements which had yet been instituted. Their distinctive feature was self-government, to which they owed their steadily increasing prosperity. No other European colonies were thus managed on the principle of autonomy. Indeed, these English settlements were in 1650 the only self-governing lands in the world, apart from England herself, the United Provinces, and Switzerland.

The first English colony, Virginia, was planted in 1608 by a trading company organised for the purpose, whose subscribers included nearly all the London City Companies, and about seven hundred private individuals of all ranks. Their motives were partly political ('to put a bit in the ancient enemy's (Spain's) mouth'), and partly commercial, for they hoped to find gold, and to render England independent of the marine supplies which came from the Baltic. But profit was not their sole aim; they were moved also by the desire to plant a new England beyond the seas. They made, in fact, no profits; but they did create a branch of the English stock, and the young squires' and yeomen's sons who formed the backbone of the colony showed themselves to be Englishmen by their unwillingness to submit to an uncontrolled direction of their affairs. In 1619, acting on instructions received from England, the company's governor summoned an assembly of representatives, one from each township, to consult on the needs of the colony. This was the first representative body that had ever existed outside Europe, and it indicated what was to be the character of English colonisation. Henceforth the normal English method of governing a colony was through a governor and an executive council appointed by the Crown or its delegate, and a representative assembly, which wielded full control over local legislation and taxation. 'Our present happiness,' said the Virginian Assembly in 1640, 'is exemplified by the freedom of annual assemblies and by legal trials by juries in all civil and criminal causes.'

The second group of English colonies, those of New England, far to the north of Virginia, reproduced in an intensified form this note of self-government. Founded in the years following 1620, these settlements were the outcome of Puritan discontents in England. The commercial motive was altogether subsidiary in their establishment; they existed in order that the doctrine and discipline of Puritanism might find a home where its ascendancy would be secure. It was indeed under the guise of a commercial company that the chief of these settlements was made, but the company was organised as a means of safe-guarding the colonists from Crown interference, and at an early date its headquarters were transferred to New England itself. Far from desiring to restrict this freedom, the Crown up to a point encouraged it. Winthrop, one of the leading colonists, tells us that he had learnt from members of the Privy Council 'that his Majesty did not intend to impose the ceremonies of the Church of England upon us; for that it was considered that it was the freedom from such things that made people come over to us.' The contrast between this licence and the rigid orthodoxy enforced upon French Canada or Spanish America is very instructive. It meant that the New World, so far as it was controlled by England, was to be open as a place of refuge for those who disliked the restrictions thought necessary at home. The same note is to be found in the colony of Maryland, planted by the Roman Catholic Lord Baltimore in 1632, largely as a place of refuge for his co-religionists. He was encouraged by the government of Charles I. in this idea, and the second Lord Baltimore reports that his father 'had absolute liberty to carry over any from his Majesty's Dominions willing to go. But he found very few but such as ... could not conform to the laws of England relating to religion. These declared themselves willing to plant in this province, if they might have a general toleration settled by law.' Maryland, therefore, became the first place in the world of Western civilisation in which full religious toleration was allowed; for the aim of the New Englanders was not religious freedom, but a free field for the rigid enforcement of their own shade of orthodoxy.

Thus, in these first English settlements, the deliberate encouragement of varieties of type was from the outset a distinguishing note, and the home authorities neither desired nor attempted to impose a strict uniformity with the rules and methods existing in England. There was as great a variety in social and economic organisation as in religious beliefs between the aristocratic planter colonies of the south and the democratic agricultural settlements of New England. In one thing only was there uniformity: every settlement possessed self-governing institutions, and prized them beyond all other privileges. None, indeed, carried self-government to so great an extent as the New Englanders. They came out organised as religious congregations, in which every member possessed equal rights, and they took the congregational system as the basis of their local government, and church membership as the test of citizenship; nor did any other colonies attain the right, long exercised by the New Englanders, of electing their own governors. But there was no English settlement, not even the little slave-worked plantations in the West Indian islands, like Barbados, which did not set up, as a matter of course, a representative body to deal with problems of legislation and taxation, and the home government never dreamt of interfering with this practice. Already in 1650, the English empire was sharply differentiated from the Spanish, the Dutch, and the French empires by the fact that it consisted of a scattered group of self-governing communities, varying widely in type, but united especially by the common possession of free institutions, and thriving very largely because these institutions enabled local needs to be duly considered and attracted settlers of many types.

(b) The Period of Systematic Colonial Policy, 1660-1713

The second half of the seventeenth century was a period of systematic imperial policy on the part of both England and France; for both countries now realised that in the profitable field of commerce, at any rate, the Dutch had won a great advantage over them.

France, after many internal troubles and many foreign wars, had at last achieved, under the government of Louis XIV., the boon of firmly established order. She was now beyond all rivalry the greatest of the European states, and her king and his great finance minister, Colbert, resolved to win for her also supremacy in trade and colonisation. But this was to be done absolutely under the control and direction of the central government. Until the establishment of the German Empire, there has never been so marked an instance of the centralised organisation of the whole national activity as France presented in this period. The French East India Company was revived under government direction, and began for the first time to be a serious competitor for Indian trade. An attempt was made to conquer Madagascar as a useful base for Eastern enterprises. The sugar industry in the French West Indian islands was scientifically encouraged and developed, though the full results of this work were not apparent until the next century. France began to take an active share in the West African trade in slaves and other commodities. In Canada a new era of prosperity began; the population was rapidly increased by the dispatch of carefully selected parties of emigrants, and the French activity in missionary work and in exploration became bolder than ever. Pere Marquette and the Sieur de la Salle traced out the courses of the Ohio and the Mississippi; French trading-stations began to arise among the scattered Indian tribes who alone occupied the vast central plain; and a strong French claim was established to the possession of this vital area, which was not only the most valuable part of the American continent, but would have shut off the English coastal settlements from any possibility of westward expansion. These remarkable explorations led, in 1717, to the foundation of New Orleans at the mouth of the great river, and the organisation of the colony of Louisiana. But the whole of the intense and systematic imperial activity of the French during this period depended upon the support and direction of government; and when Colbert died in 1683, and soon afterwards all the resources of France were strained by the pressure of two great European wars, the rapid development which Colbert's zeal had brought about was checked for a generation. Centralised administration may produce remarkable immediate results, but it does not encourage natural and steady growth. Meanwhile the English had awakened to the fact that England had, almost by a series of accidents, become the centre of an empire, and to the necessity of giving to this empire some sort of systematic organisation. It was the statesmen of the Commonwealth who first began to grope after an imperial system. The aspect of the situation which most impressed them was that the enterprising Dutch were reaping most of the trading profits which arose from the creation of the English colonies: it was said that ten Dutch ships called at Barbados for every English ship. To deal with this they passed the Navigation Act of 1651, which provided that the trade of England and the colonies should be carried only in English or colonial ships. They thus gave a logical expression to the policy of imperial trade monopoly which had been in the minds of those who were interested in colonial questions from the outset; and they also opened a period of acute trade rivalry and war with the Dutch. The first of the Dutch wars, which was waged by the Commonwealth, was a very even struggle, but it secured the success of the Navigation Act. Cromwell, though he hastened to make peace with the Dutch, was a still stronger imperialist than his parliamentary predecessors; he may justly be described as the first of the Jingoes. He demanded compensation from the Dutch for the half-forgotten outrage of Amboyna in 1623. He made a quite unprovoked attack upon the Spanish island of Hispaniola, and though he failed to conquer it, gained a compensation in the seizure of Jamaica (1655). And he insisted upon the obedience of the colonies to the home government with a severity never earlier shown. With him imperial aims may be said to have become, for the first time, one of the ruling ends of the English government.

But it was the reign of Charles II. which saw the definite organisation of a clearly conceived imperial policy; in the history of English imperialism there are few periods more important. The chief statesmen and courtiers of the reign, Prince Rupert, Clarendon, Shaftesbury, Albemarle, were all enthusiasts for the imperial idea. They had a special committee of the Privy Council for Trade and Plantations,[4] and appointed John Locke, the ablest political thinker of the age, to be its secretary. They pushed home the struggle against the maritime ascendancy of the Dutch, and fought two Dutch wars; and though the history-books, influenced by the Whig prejudice against Charles II., always treat these wars as humiliating and disgraceful, while they treat the Dutch war of the Commonwealth as just and glorious, the plain fact is that the first Dutch war of Charles II. led to the conquest of the Dutch North American colony of the New Netherlands (1667), and so bridged the gap between the New England and the southern colonies. They engaged in systematic colonisation, founding the new colony of Carolina to the south of Virginia, while out of their Dutch conquests they organised the colonies of New York, New Jersey, and Delaware; and the end of the reign saw the establishment of the interesting and admirably managed Quaker colony of Pennsylvania. They started the Hudson Bay Company, which engaged in the trade in furs to the north of the French colonies. They systematically encouraged the East India Company, which now began to be more prosperous than at any earlier period, and obtained in Bombay its first territorial possession in India.

[4] It was not till 1696, however, that this Board became permanent.

More important, they worked out a new colonial policy, which was to remain, in its main features, the accepted British policy down to the loss of the American colonies in 1782. The theory at the base of this policy was that while the mother-country must be responsible for the defence of all the scattered settlements, which in their weakness were exposed to attack from many sides, in she might reasonably expect to be put in possession of definite trade advantages. Hence the Navigation Act of 1660 provided not only that inter-imperial trade should be carried in English or colonial vessels, but that certain 'enumerated articles,' including some of the most important colonial products, should be sent only to England, so that English merchants should have the profits of selling them to other countries, and the English government the proceeds of duties upon them; and another Act provided that imports to the colonies should only come from, or through, England. In other words, England was to be the commercial entrepot of the whole empire; and the regulation of imperial trade as a whole was to belong to the English government and parliament. To the English government also must necessarily fall the conduct of the relations of the empire as a whole with other powers. This commercial system was not, however, purely one-sided. If the colonies were to send their chief products only to England, they were at the same time to have a monopoly, or a marked advantage, in English markets. Tobacco-growing had been for a time a promising industry in England; it was prohibited in order that it might not compete with the colonial product; and differential duties were levied on the competing products of other countries and their colonies. In short, the new policy was one of Imperial Preference; it aimed at turning the empire into an economic unit, of which England should be the administrative and distributing centre. So far the English policy did not differ in kind from the contemporary colonial policy of other countries, though it left to the colonies a greater freedom of trade (for example, in the 'non-enumerated articles') than was ever allowed by Spain or France, or by the two great trading companies which controlled the foreign possessions of Holland.

But there is one respect in which the authors of this system differed very widely from the colonial statesmen of other countries. Though they were anxious to organise and consolidate the empire on the basis of a trade system, they had no desire or intention of altering its self-governing character, or of discouraging the growth of a healthy diversity of type and method. Every one of the new colonies of this period was provided with the accustomed machinery of representative government: in the case of Carolina, the philosopher, John Locke, was invited to draw up a model constitution, and although his scheme was quite unworkable, the fact that he was asked to make it affords a striking proof of the seriousness with which the problems of colonial government were regarded. In several of the West Indian settlements self-governing institutions were organised during these years. In the Frame of Government which Penn set forth on the foundation of Pennsylvania, in 1682, he laid it down that 'any government is free where the laws rule, and where the people are a party to these rules,' and on this basis proceeded to organise his system. According to this definition all the English colonies were free, and they were almost the only free communities in the world. And though it is true that there was an almost unceasing conflict between the government and the New England colonies, no one who studies the story of these quarrels can fail to see that the demands of the New Englanders were often unreasonable and inconsistent with the maintenance of imperial unity, while the home government was extremely patient and moderate. Above all, almost the most marked feature of the colonial policy of Charles II. was the uniform insistence upon complete religious toleration in the colonies. Every new charter contained a clause securing this vital condition.

It has long been our habit to condemn the old colonial system as it was defined in this period, and to attribute to it the disruption of the empire in the eighteenth century. But the judgment is not a fair one; it is due to those Whig prejudices by which so much of the modern history of England has been distorted. The colonial policy of Shaftesbury and his colleagues was incomparably more enlightened than that of any contemporary government. It was an interesting experiment — the first, perhaps, in modern history — in the reconciliation of unity and freedom. And it was undeniably successful: under it the English colonies grew and throve in a very striking way. Everything, indeed, goes to show that this system was well designed for the needs of a group of colonies which were still in a state of weakness, still gravely under-peopled and undeveloped. Evil results only began to show themselves in the next age, when the colonies were growing stronger and more independent, and when the self-complacent Whigs, instead of revising the system to meet new conditions, actually enlarged and emphasised its most objectionable features.

(c) The Conflict of French and English, 1713-1763

While France and England were defining and developing their sharply contrasted imperial systems, the Dutch had fallen into the background, content with the rich dominion which they had already acquired; and the Spanish and Portuguese empires had both fallen into stagnation. New competitors, indeed, now began to press into the field: the wildly exaggerated notions of the wealth to be made from colonial ventures which led to the frenzied speculations of the early eighteenth century, John Law's schemes, and the South Sea Bubble, induced other powers to try to obtain a share of this wealth; and Austria, Brandenburg, and Denmark made fitful endeavours to become colonising powers. But the enterprises of these states were never of serious importance. The future of the non-European world seemed to depend mainly upon France and England; and it was yet to be determined which of the two systems, centralised autocracy enforcing uniformity, or self-government encouraging variety of type, would prove the more successful and would play the greater part. Two bodies of ideas so sharply contrasted were bound to come into conflict. In the two great wars between England and Louis XIV. (1688-1713), though the questions at issue were primarily European, the conflict inevitably spread to the colonial field; and in the result France was forced to cede in 1713 the province of Acadia (which had twice before been in English hands), the vast basin of Hudson's Bay, and the island of Newfoundland, to which the fishermen of both nations had resorted, though the English had always claimed it. But these were only preliminaries, and the main conflict was fought out during the half-century following the Peace of Utrecht, 1713-63.

During this half-century Britain was under the rule of the Whig oligarchy, which had no clearly conceived ideas on imperial policy. Under the influence of the mercantile class the Whigs increased the severity of the restrictions on colonial trade, and prohibited the rise of industries likely to compete with those of the mother-country. But under the influence of laziness and timidity, and of the desire quieta non movere, they made no attempt seriously to enforce either the new or the old restrictions, and in these circumstances smuggling trade between the New England colonies and the French West Indies, in defiance of the Navigation Act and its companions, grew to such dimensions that any serious interference with it would be felt as a real grievance. The Whigs and their friends later took credit for their neglect. George Grenville, they said, lost the colonies because he read the American dispatches; he would have done much better to leave the dispatches and the colonies alone. But this is a damning apology. If the old colonial system, whose severity, on paper, the Whigs had greatly increased, was no longer workable, it should have been revised; but no Whig showed any sign of a sense that change was necessary. Yet the prevalence of smuggling was not the only proof of the need for change. There was during the period a long succession of disputes between colonial governors and their assemblies, which showed that the restrictions upon their political freedom, as well as those upon their economic freedom, were beginning to irk the colonists; and that self-government was following its universal and inevitable course, and demanding its own fulfilment. But the Whigs made no sort of attempt to consider the question whether the self-government of the colonies could be increased without impairing the unity of the empire. The single device of their statesmanship was—not to read the dispatches. And, in the meanwhile, no evil results followed, because the loyalty of the colonists was ensured by the imminence of the French danger. The mother-country was still responsible for the provision of defence, though she was largely cheated of the commercial advantages which were to have been its recompense.

After 1713 there was a comparatively long interval of peace between Britain and France, but it was occupied by an acute commercial rivalry, in which, on the whole, the French seemed to be getting the upper hand. Their sugar islands in the West Indies were more productive than the British; their traders were rapidly increasing their hold over the central plain of North America, to the alarm of the British colonists; their intrigues kept alive a perpetual unrest in the recently conquered province of Acadia; and away in India, under the spirited direction of Francois Dupleix, their East India Company became a more formidable competitor for the Indian trade than it had hitherto been. Hence the imperial problem presented itself to the statesmen of that generation as a problem of power rather than as a problem of organisation; and the intense rivalry with France dwarfed and obscured the need for a reconsideration of colonial relations. At length this rivalry flamed out into two wars. The first of these was fought, on both sides, in a strangely half-hearted and lackadaisical way. But in the second (the Seven Years' War, 1756-63) the British cause, after two years of disaster, fell under the confident and daring leadership of Pitt, which brought a series of unexampled successes. The French flag was almost swept from the seas. The French settlements in Canada were overrun and conquered. With the fall of Quebec it was determined that the system of self-government, and not that of autocracy, should control the destinies of the North American continent; and Britain emerged in 1763 the supreme colonial power of the world. The problem of power had been settled in her favour; but the problem of organisation remained unsolved. It emerged in an acute and menacing form as soon as the war was over.

During the course of these two wars, and in the interval between them, an extraordinary series of events had opened a new scene for the rivalry of the two great imperial powers, and a new world began to be exposed to the influence of the political ideas of Europe. The vast and populous land of India, where the Europeans had hitherto been content to play the part of modest traders, under the protection and control of great native rulers, had suddenly been displayed as a field for the imperial ambitions of the European peoples. Ever since the first appearance of the Dutch, the English, and the French in these regions, Northern India had formed a consolidated empire ruled from Delhi by the great Mogul dynasty; the shadow of its power was also cast over the lesser princes of Southern India. But after 1709, and still more after 1739, the Mogul Empire collapsed, and the whole of India, north and south, rapidly fell into a condition of complete anarchy. A multitude of petty rulers, nominal satraps of the powerless Mogul, roving adventurers, or bands of Mahratta raiders, put an end to all order and security; and to protect themselves and maintain their trade the European traders must needs enlist considerable bodies of Indian troops. It had long been proved that a comparatively small number of troops, disciplined in the European fashion, could hold their own against the loose and disorderly mobs who followed the standards of Indian rulers. And it now occurred to the ambitious mind of the Frenchman Dupleix that it should be possible, by the use of this military superiority, to intervene with effect in the unceasing strife of the Indian princes, to turn the scale on one side or the other, and to obtain over the princes whose cause he embraced a commanding influence, which would enable him to secure the expulsion of his English rivals, and the establishment of a French trade monopoly based upon political influence.

This daring project was at first triumphantly successful. The English had to follow suit in self-defence, but could not equal the ability of Dupleix. In 1750 a French protege occupied the most important throne of Southern India at Hyderabad, and was protected and kept loyal by a force of French sepoys under the Marquis de Bussy, whose expenses were met out of the revenues of large provinces (the Northern Sarkars) placed under French administration; while in the Carnatic, the coastal region where all the European traders had their south-eastern headquarters, a second French protege had almost succeeded in crushing his rival, whom the English company supported. But the genius of Clive reversed the situation with dramatic swiftness; the French authorities at home, alarmed at these dangerous adventures, repudiated and recalled Dupleix (1754), and the British power was left to apply the methods which he had invented. When the Seven Years' War broke out (1756), the French, repenting of their earlier decision, sent a substantial force to restore their lost influence in the Carnatic, but the result was complete failure. A British protege henceforward ruled in the Carnatic; a British force replaced the French at Hyderabad; and the revenues of the Northern Sarkars, formerly assigned for the maintenance of the French force, were handed over to its successor. Meanwhile in the rich province of Bengal a still more dramatic revolution had taken place. Attacked by the young Nawab, Siraj-uddaula, the British traders at Calcutta had been forced to evacuate that prosperous centre (1756). But Clive, coming up with a fleet and an army from Madras, applied the lessons he had learnt in the Carnatic, set up a rival claimant to the throne of Bengal, and at Plassey (1757) won for his puppet a complete victory. From 1757 onwards the British East India Company was the real master in Bengal, even more completely than in the Carnatic. It had not, in either region, conquered any territory; it had only supported successfully a claimant to the native throne. The native government, in theory, continued as before; the company, in theory, was its subject and vassal. But in practice these great and rich provinces lay at its mercy, and if it did not yet choose to undertake their government, this was only because it preferred to devote itself to its original business of trade.

Thus by 1763 the British power had achieved a dazzling double triumph. It had destroyed the power of its chief rival both in the East and in the West. It had established the supremacy of the British peoples and of British methods of government throughout the whole continent of North America; and it had entered, blindly and without any conception of what the future was to bring forth, upon the path which was to lead to dominion over the vast continent of India, and upon the tremendous task of grafting the ideas of the West upon the East.

Such was the outcome of the first two periods in the history of European imperialism. It left Central and South America under the stagnant and reactionary government of Spain and Portugal; the eastern coast of North America under the control of groups of self-governing Englishmen; Canada, still inhabited by Frenchmen, under British dominance; Java and the Spice Islands, together with the small settlement of Cape Colony, in the hands of the Dutch; a medley of European settlements in the West Indian islands, and a string of European factories along the coast of West Africa; and the beginning of an anomalous British dominion established at two points on the coast of India. But of all the European nations which had taken part in this vast process of expansion, one alone, the British, still retained its vitality and its expansive power.

IV
THE ERA OF REVOLUTION, 1763-1825

'Colonies are like fruits,' said Turgot, the eighteenth-century French economist and statesman: 'they cling to the mother-tree only until they are ripe.' This generalisation, which represented a view very widely held during that and the next age, seemed to be borne out in the most conclusive way by the events of the sixty years following the Seven Years' War. In 1763 the French had lost almost the whole of the empire which they had toilsomely built up during a century and a half. Within twenty years their triumphant British rivals were forced to recognise the independence of the American colonies, and thus lost the bulk of what may be called the first British Empire. They still retained the recently conquered province of French Canada, but it seemed unlikely that the French Canadians would long be content to live under an alien dominion: if they had not joined in the American Revolution, it was not because they loved the British, but because they hated the Americans. The French Revolutionary wars brought further changes. One result of these wars was that the Dutch lost Cape Colony, Ceylon, and Java, though Java was restored to them in 1815. A second result was that when Napoleon made himself master of Spain in 1808, the Spanish colonies in Central and South America ceased to be governed from the mother-country; and having tasted the sweets of independence, and still more, the advantages of unrestricted trade, could never again be brought into subordination. By 1825 nothing was left of the vast Spanish Empire save the Canaries, Cuba, Porto Rico, and the Philippine Islands; nothing was left of the Portuguese Empire save a few decaying posts on the coasts of Africa and India; nothing was left of the Dutch Empire save Java and its dependencies, restored in 1815; nothing was left of the French Empire save a few West Indian islands; and what had been the British American colonies were now the United States, a great power declaring to Europe, through the mouth of President Monroe, that she would resist any attempt of the European powers to restore the old regime in South America. It appeared that the political control of European states over non-European regions must be short-lived and full of trouble; and that the influence of Europe upon the non-European world would henceforth be exercised mainly through new independent states imbued with European ideas. Imperial aspirations thus seemed to that and the next generation at once futile and costly.

Of all these colonial revolutions the most striking was that which tore away the American colonies from Britain (1764-82); not only because it led to the creation of one of the great powers of the world, and was to afford the single instance which has yet arisen of a daughter-nation outnumbering its mother-country, but still more because it seemed to prove that not even the grant of extensive powers of self-government would secure the permanent loyalty of colonies. Indeed, from the standpoint of Realpolitik, it might be argued that in the case of America self-government was shown to be a dangerous gift; for the American colonies, which alone among European settlements had obtained this supreme endowment, were the first, and indeed the only, European settlements to throw off deliberately their connection with the mother-country. France and Holland lost their colonies by war, and even the Spanish colonies would probably never have thought of severing their relations with Spain but for the anomalous conditions created by the Napoleonic conquest.

The American Revolution is, then, an event unique at once in its causes, its character, and its consequences; and it throws a most important illumination upon some of the problems of imperialism. It cannot be pretended that the revolt of the colonists was due to oppression or to serious misgovernment. The paltry taxes which were its immediate provoking cause would have formed a quite negligible burden upon a very prosperous population; they were to have been spent exclusively within the colonies themselves, and would have been mainly used to meet a part of the cost of colonial defence, the bulk of which was still to be borne by the mother-country. If the colonists had been willing to suggest any other means of raising the required funds, their suggestions would have been readily accepted. This was made plain at several stages in the course of the discussion, but the invitation to suggest alternative methods of raising money met with no response. The plain fact is that Britain, already heavily loaded with debt, was bearing practically the whole burden of colonial defence, and was much less able than the colonies themselves to endure the strain. As for the long-established restrictions on colonial trade, which in fact though not in form contributed as largely as the proposals of direct taxation to cause the revolt, they were far less severe, even if they had been strictly enforced, than the restrictions imposed upon the trade of other European settlements.

It is equally misleading to attribute the blame of the revolt wholly to George III. and the ministers by whom he was served during the critical years. No doubt it is possible to imagine a more tactful man than George Grenville, a more far-seeing and courageous statesman than Lord North, a less obstinate prince than George III. himself. But it may be doubted whether any change of men would have done more than postpone the inevitable. The great Whig apologists who have dictated the accepted view of British history in the seventeenth and eighteenth centuries have laboured to create the impression that if only Burke, Chatham, and Charles Fox had had the handling of the issue, the tragedy of disruption would have been avoided. But there is no evidence that any of these men, except perhaps Burke, appreciated the magnitude and difficulty of the questions that had been inevitably raised in 1764, and must have been raised whoever had been in power; or that they would have been able to suggest a workable new scheme of colonial government which would have met the difficulty. If they had put forward such a scheme, it would have been wrecked on the resistance of British opinion, which was still dominated by the theories and traditions of the old colonial system; and even if it had overcome this obstacle, it would very likely have been ruined by the captious and litigious spirit to which events had given birth among the colonists, especially in New England.

The root of the matter was that the old colonial system, which had suited well enough the needs of the colonies as they were when it was devised by the statesmen of Charles II.'s reign, was no longer suitable to their condition now that they had become great and prosperous communities of freemen. They enjoyed self-government on a scale more generous than any other communities in the world outside of Britain; indeed, in one sense they enjoyed it on a more generous scale than Britain herself, since political rights were much more widely exercised in the colonies, owing to the natural conditions of a new and prosperous land, than they were to be, or could be, in Britain until nearly a century later. No direct taxation had as yet been imposed upon them without their own consent. They made the laws by which their own lives were regulated. They were called upon to pay no tribute to the home government, except the very indirect levy on goods passing through England to or from their ports, and this was nearly balanced by the advantages which they enjoyed in the British market, and far more than balanced by the protection afforded to them by the British fleet. They were not even required to raise troops for the defence of their own frontiers except of their own free will, and the main burden of defending even their landward frontier was borne by the mother-country. But being British they had the instinct of self-government in their blood and bones, and they found that the control of their own affairs was qualified or limited in two principal ways.

In the first place, the executive and judicial officers who carried out the laws were not appointed by them but by the Crown in England: the colonies were not responsible for the administration of their own laws. In the second place, the regulations by which their foreign trade was governed were determined, not by themselves, but by the British parliament: they were not responsible for the control of their own traffic with the outside world. It is true that the salaries of the executive officials and the judges depended upon their grant, and that any governor who acted in the teeth of colonial opinion would find his position quite untenable, so that the colonists exercised a real if indirect control over administration. It is true also that they accepted the general principles of the commercial system, and had reaped great benefits from it.

But it is the unfailing instinct of the citizens in a self-governing community to be dissatisfied unless they feel that they have a full and equal share in the control of their own destinies. Denied responsibility, they are apt to become irresponsible; and when all allowance has been made for the stupidities of governors and for the mistakes of the home authorities, it must be recognised that the thirteen American colonial legislatures often behaved in a very irresponsible way, and were extremely difficult to handle. They refused to vote fixed salaries to their judges in order to make their power felt, simply because the judges were appointed by the Crown, although in doing so they were dangerously undermining judicial independence. They refused in many cases to supply anything like adequate contingents for the war against the French and their Indian allies, partly because each legislature was afraid of being more generous than the others, partly because they could trust to the home government to make good their deficiencies. Yet at the same time they did nothing to check, but rather encouraged, the wholesale smuggling by which the trade regulations were reduced to a nullity, though these regulations were not only accepted in principle by themselves, but afforded the only compensation to the mother-country for the cost of colonial defence. It is as unscientific to blame the colonists and their legislatures for this kind of action, as it is to blame the British statesmen for their proposals. It was the almost inevitable result of the conditions among a free, prosperous, and extremely self-confident people; it was, indeed, the proof that in this young people the greatest political ideal of western civilisation, the ideal of self-government, had taken firm root. The denial of responsibility was producing irresponsibility; and even if the Stamp Act and the Tea Duties had never been proposed, this state of things was bound to lead to increasing friction. Nor must it be forgotten that this friction was accentuated by the contrast between the democratic conditions of colonial life, and the aristocratic organisation of English society.

It ought to have been obvious, long before Grenville initiated his new policy in 1764, that the colonial system was not working well; and the one circumstance which had prevented serious conflict was the danger which threatened the colonists in the aggressive attitude of the French to the north and west. Since the individual colonies refused to raise adequate forces for their own defence, or to co-operate with one another in a common scheme, they were dependent for their security upon the mother-country. But as soon as the danger was removed, as it was in 1763, this reason for restraint vanished; and although the great majority of the colonists were quite sincerely desirous of retaining their membership of the British commonwealth, the conditions would inevitably have produced a state of intensifying friction, unless the whole colonial system had been drastically reconstructed.

Reconstruction was therefore inevitable in 1764. The Whig policy of simply ignoring the issue and 'not reading the dispatches' could no longer be pursued; it was indeed largely responsible for the mischief. George III. and Grenville deserve the credit of seeing this. But their scheme of reconstruction not unnaturally amounted to little more than a tightening-up of the old system. The trade laws were to be more strictly enforced. The governors and the judges were to be made more independent of the assemblies by being given fixed salaries. The colonists were to bear a larger share of the cost of defence, which fell so unfairly on the mother-country. If the necessary funds could be raised by means approved by the colonists themselves, well and good; but if not, then they must be raised by the authority of the imperial parliament. For the existing system manifestly could not continue indefinitely, and it was better to have the issue clearly raised, even at the risk of conflict, than to go on merely drifting.

When the colonists (without suggesting any alternative proposals) contented themselves with repudiating the right of parliament to tax them, and proceeded to outrageous insults to the king's authority, and the most open defiance of the trade regulations, indignation grew in Britain. It seemed, to the average Englishman, that the colonists proposed to leave every public burden, even the cost of judges' salaries, on the shoulders of the mother-country, already loaded with a debt which had been largely incurred in defence of the colonies; but to disregard every obligation imposed upon themselves. A system whereunder the colony has all rights and no enforcible duties, the mother-country all duties and no enforcible rights, obviously could not work. That was the system which, in the view of the gentlemen of England, the colonists were bent upon establishing; and, taking this view, they cannot be blamed for refusing to accept such a conclusion. There was no one, either in Britain or in America, capable of grasping the essentials of the problem, which were that, once established, self-government inevitably strives after its own fulfilment; that these British settlers, in whom the British tradition of self-government had been strengthened by the freedom of a new land, would never be content until they enjoyed a full share in the control of their own affairs; and that although they seemed, even to themselves, to be fighting about legal minutiae, about the difference between internal and external duties, about the legality of writs of assistance, and so forth, the real issue was the deeper one of the fulfilment of self-government. Could fully responsible self-government be reconciled with imperial unity? Could any means be devised whereby the units in a fellowship of free states might retain full control over their own affairs, and at the same time effectively combine for common purposes? That was and is the ultimate problem of British imperial organisation, as it was and is the ultimate problem of international relations. But the problem, though it now presented itself in a comparatively simple form, was never fairly faced on either side of the Atlantic. For the mother and her daughters too quickly reached the point of arguing about their legal rights against one another, and when friends begin to argue about their legal rights, the breach of their friendship is at hand. So the dreary argument, which lasted for eleven years (1764-75), led to the still more dreary war, which lasted for seven years (1775-82); and the only family of free self-governing communities existing in the world was broken up in bitterness. This was indeed a tragedy. For if the great partnership of freedom could have been reorganised on conditions that would have enabled it to hold together, the cause of liberty in the world would have been made infinitely more secure.

The Revolution gave to the Americans the glory of establishing the first fully democratic system of government on a national scale that had yet existed in the world, and of demonstrating that by the machinery of self-government a number of distinct and jealous communities could be united for common purposes. The new American Commonwealth became an inspiration for eager Liberals in the old world as well as in the new, and its successful establishment formed the strongest of arguments for the democratic idea in all lands. Unhappily the pride of this great achievement helped to persuade the Americans that they were different from the rest of the world, and unaffected by its fortunes. They were apt to think of themselves as the inventors and monopolists of political liberty. Cut off by a vast stretch of ocean from the Old World, and having lost that contact with its affairs which the relation with Britain had hitherto maintained, they followed but dimly, and without much comprehension, the obscure and complex struggles wherein the spirit of liberty was working out a new Europe, in the face of difficulties vastly greater than any with which the Americans had ever had to contend. They had been alienated from Britain, the one great free state of Europe, and had been persuaded by their reading of their own experience that she was a tyrant-power; and they thus found it hard to recognise her for what, with all her faults, she genuinely was—the mother of free institutions in the modern world, the founder and shaper of their own prized liberties. All these things combined to persuade the great new republic that she not only might, but ought to, stand aloof from the political problems of the rest of the world, and take no interest in its concerns. This attitude, the natural product of the conditions, was to last for more than a century, and was to weaken greatly the cause of liberty in the world.

Although the most obvious features of the half-century following the great British triumph of 1763 were the revolt of the American colonies and the apparently universal collapse of the imperialist ambitions of the European nations, a more deeply impressive feature of the period was that, in spite of the tragedy and humiliation of the great disruption, the imperial impetus continued to work potently in Britain, alone among the European nations; and to such effect that at the end of the period she found herself in control of a new empire more extensive than that which she had lost, and far more various in its character. Having failed to solve one great imperial problem, she promptly addressed herself to a whole series of others even more difficult, and for these she was to find more hopeful solutions.

When the American revolt began, the Canadian colonies to the north were in an insecure and unorganised state. On the coast, in Nova Scotia and Newfoundland, there was a small British population; but the riverine colony of Canada proper, with its centre at Quebec, was still purely French, and was ruled by martial law. Accustomed to a despotic system, and not yet reconciled to the British supremacy, the French settlers were obviously unready for self-government. But the Quebec Act of 1774, by securing the maintenance of the Roman Catholic religion and of French civil law, ensured the loyalty of the French; and this Act is also noteworthy as the first formal expression of willingness to admit or even welcome the existence, within the hospitable limits of the Empire, of a variety of types of civilisation. In the new British Empire there was to be no uniformity of Kultur.

The close of the American struggle, however, brought a new problem. Many thousands of exiles from the revolting colonies, willing to sacrifice everything in order to retain their British citizenship, poured over the borders into the Canadian lands. They settled for the first time the rich province of Ontario, greatly increased the population of Nova Scotia, and started the settlement of New Brunswick. To these exiles Britain felt that she owed much, and, despite her own financial distress, expended large sums in providing them with the means to make a good beginning in their new homes. But it was impossible to deny these British settlers, and the emigrants from Britain who soon began to join them, the rights of self-government, to which they were accustomed. Their advent, however, in a hitherto French province, raised the very difficult problem of racial relationship. They might have been used as a means for Anglicising the earlier French settlers and for forcing them into a British mould; it may fairly be said that most European governments would have used them in this way, and many of the settlers would willingly have fallen in with such a programme. But that would have been out of accord with the genius of the British system, which believes in freedom and variety. Accordingly, by the Act of 1791, the purely French region of Quebec or Lower Canada was separated from the British region of Ontario or Upper Canada, and both districts, as well as the coastal settlements, were endowed with self-governing institutions of the familiar pattern—an elected assembly controlling legislation and taxation, a nominated governor and council directing the executive. Thus within eighteen years of their conquest the French colonists were introduced to self-government. And within nine years of the loss of the American colonies, a new group of self-governing American colonies had been organised. They were sufficiently content with the system to resist with vigour and success an American invasion in 1812. While the American controversy was proceeding, one of the greatest of British navigators, Captain Cook, was busy with his remarkable explorations. He was the first to survey the archipelagoes of the Pacific; more important, he was the real discoverer of Australia and New Zealand; for though the Dutch explorers had found these lands more than a century earlier, they had never troubled to complete their explorations. Thus a vast new field, eminently suitable for European settlement, was placed at the disposal of Britain. It was utilised with extraordinary promptitude. The loss of the American colonies had deprived Britain of her chief dumping-ground for convicts. In 1788, six years after the recognition of their independence, she decided to use the new continent for this purpose, and the penal settlement of Botany Bay began (under unfavourable auspices) the colonisation of Australia.

But the most important, and the most amazing, achievement of Britain in this period was the establishment and extension of her empire in India, and the planting within it of the first great gift of Western civilisation, the sovereignty of a just and impartial law. This was a novel and a very difficult task, such as no European people had yet undertaken; and it is not surprising that there should have been a period of bewildered misgovernment before it was achieved. That it should have been achieved at all is one of the greatest miracles of European imperialism.

By 1763 the East India Company had established a controlling influence over the Nawabs of two important regions, Bengal and the Carnatic, and had shown, in a series of struggles, that its control was not to be shaken off. But the company had not annexed any territory, or assumed any responsibility for the government of these rich provinces. Its agents in the East, who were too far from London to be effectively controlled, enjoyed power without responsibility. They were privileged traders, upon whom the native governments dared not impose restrictions, and (as any body of average men would have done under similar circumstances) they gravely abused their position to build up huge fortunes for themselves. During the fifteen years following the battle of Plassey (1757) there is no denying that the political power of the British in India was a mere curse to the native population, and led to the complete disorganisation of the already decrepit native system of government in the provinces affected. It was vain for the directors at home to scold their servants. There were only two ways out of the difficulty. One was that the company should abandon India, which was not to be expected. The other was that, possessing power, of which it was now impossible to strip themselves, they should assume the responsibility for its exercise, and create for their subjects a just and efficient system of government. But the company would not see this. They had never desired political power, but had drifted into the possession of it in spite of themselves. They honestly disliked the idea of establishing by force an alien domination over subject peoples, and this feeling was yet more strongly held by the most influential political circles in England. The company desired nothing but trade. Their business was that of traders, and they wanted only to be left free to mind their business. So the evils arising from power without responsibility continued, and half-hearted attempts to amend them in 1765 and in 1769 only made the conditions worse. The events of the years from 1757 to 1772 showed that when the superior organisation of the West came in contact with the East, mere trading exploitation led to even worse results than a forcibly imposed dominion; and the only solution lay in the wise adaptation of western methods of government to eastern conditions.

Thus Britain found herself faced with an imperial problem of apparently insuperable difficulty, which reached its most acute stage just at the time when the American trouble was at its height. The British parliament and government intervened, and in 1773 for the first time assumed some responsibility for the affairs of the East India Company. But they did not understand the Indian problem — how, indeed, should they? — and their first solution was a failure. By a happy fortune, however, the East India Company had conferred the governorship of Bengal (1772) upon the greatest Englishman of the eighteenth century, Warren Hastings. Hastings pensioned off the Nawab, took over direct responsibility for the government of Bengal, and organised a system of justice which, though far from perfect, established for the first time the Reign of Law in an Indian realm. His firm and straightforward dealings with the other Indian powers still further strengthened the position of the company; and when in the midst of the American war, at a moment when no aid could be expected from Britain, a combination of the most formidable Indian powers, backed by a French fleet, threatened the downfall of the company's authority, Hastings' resourceful and inspiring leadership was equal to every emergency. He not only brought the company with heightened prestige out of the war, but throughout its course no hostile army was ever allowed to cross the frontiers of Bengal. In the midst of the unceasing and desolating wars of India, the territories under direct British rule formed an island of secure peace and of justice. That was Hastings' supreme contribution: it was the foundation upon which arose the fabric of the Indian Empire. Hastings was not a great conqueror or annexer of territory; the only important acquisition made during his regime was effected, in defiance of his protests, by the hostile majority which for a time overrode him in his own council, and which condemned him for ambition. His work was to make the British rule mean security and justice in place of tyranny; and it was because it had come to mean this that it grew, after his time, with extraordinary rapidity.

It was not by the desire of the directors or the home government that it grew. They did everything in their power to check its growth, for they shrank from any increase to their responsibilities. They even prohibited by law all annexations, or the making of alliances with Indian powers.[5] But fate was too strong for them. Even a governor like Lord Cornwallis, a convinced supporter of the policy of non-expansion and non-intervention, found himself forced into war, and compelled to annex territories; because non-intervention was interpreted by the Indian powers as a confession of weakness and an invitation to attack. Non-intervention also gave openings to the French, who, since the outbreak of the Revolution, had revived their old Indian ambitions; and while Bonaparte was engaged in the conquest of Egypt as a half-way house to India (1797), French agents were busy building up a new combination of Indian powers against the company.

[5] India Act of 1784

This formidable coalition was about to come to a head when, in 1798, there landed in India a second man of genius, sent by fate at the critical moment. In five years, by an amazing series of swiftly successful wars and brilliantly conceived treaties, the Marquess Wellesley broke the power of every member of the hostile coalitions, except two of the Mahratta princes. The area of British territory was quadrupled; the most important of the Indian princes became vassals of the company; and the Great Mogul of Delhi himself, powerless now, but always a symbol of the over-lordship of India, passed under British protection. When Wellesley left India in 1805, the East India Company was already the paramount power in India south-east of the Sutlej and the Indus. The Mahratta princes, indeed, still retained a restricted independence, and for an interval the home authorities declined to permit any interference with them, even though they were manifestly giving protection to bands of armed raiders who terrorised and devastated territories which were under British protection. But the time came when the Mahrattas themselves broke the peace. Then their power also was broken; and in 1818 Britain stood forth as the sovereign ruler of India.

This was only sixty years after the battle of Plassey had established British influence, though not British rule, in a single province of India; only a little over thirty years after Warren Hastings returned to England, leaving behind him an empire still almost limited to that single province. There is nothing in history that can be compared with the swiftness of this achievement, which is all the more remarkable when we remember that almost every step in the advance was taken with extreme unwillingness. But the most impressive thing about this astounding fabric of power, which extended over an area equal to half of Europe and inhabited by perhaps one-sixth of the human race, was not the swiftness with which it was created, but the results which flowed from it. It had begun in corruption and oppression, but it had grown because it had come to stand for justice, order, and peace. In 1818 it could already be claimed for the British rule in India that it had brought to the numerous and conflicting races, religions, and castes of that vast and ancient land, three boons of the highest value: political unity such as they had never known before; security from the hitherto unceasing ravages of internal turbulence and war; and, above all, the supreme gift which the West had to offer to the East, the substitution of an unvarying Reign of Law for the capricious wills of innumerable and shifting despots. This is an achievement unexampled in history, and it alone justified the imposition of the rule of the West over the East, which had at first seemed to produce nothing but evil. It took place during the age of Revolution, when the external empires of Europe were on all sides falling into ruin; and it passed at the time almost unregarded, because it was overshadowed by the drama of the Revolutionary and Napoleonic Wars.

The construction of the Indian Empire would of itself suffice to make an age memorable, but it does not end the catalogue of the achievements of British imperialism in this tremendous period. As a result of the participation of Holland in the war on the side of France, the Dutch colony at the Cape of Good Hope was occupied by Britain. It was first occupied in 1798, restored for a brief period in 1801, reoccupied in 1806, and finally retained under the treaty settlement of 1815. The Cape was, in fact, the most important acquisition secured to Britain by that treaty; and it is worth noting that while the other great powers who had joined in the final overthrow of Napoleon helped themselves without hesitation to immense and valuable territories, Britain, which had alone maintained the struggle from beginning to end without flagging, actually paid the sum of 2,000,000 pounds to Holland as a compensation for this thinly peopled settlement. She retained it mainly because of its value as a calling-station on the way to India. But it imposed upon her an imperial problem of a very difficult kind. As in Canada, she had to deal here with an alien race of European origin and proud traditions; but this racial problem was accentuated by the further problem of dealing with a preponderant and growing negro population. How were justice, peace, liberty, and equality of rights to be established in such a field?

It was, then, an astonishing new empire which had grown up round Britain during the period when the world was becoming convinced that colonial empires were not worth acquiring, because they could not last. It was an empire of continents or sub-continents—Canada, Australia, India, South Africa—not to speak of innumerable scattered islands and trading-posts dotted over all the seas of the world, which had either survived from an earlier period, or been acquired in order that they might serve as naval bases. It was spread round the whole globe; it included almost every variety of soil, products, and climate; it was inhabited by peoples of the most varying types; it presented an infinite variety of political and racial problems. In 1825 this empire was the only extra-European empire of importance still controlled by any of the historic imperial powers of Western Europe. And at the opening of the nineteenth century, when extra-European empires seemed to have gone out of fashion, the greatest of all imperial questions was the question whether the political capacity of the British peoples, having failed to solve the comparatively simple problem of finding a mode of organisation which could hold together communities so closely akin as those of America and the parent islands, would be capable of achieving any land of effective organisation for this new astounding fabric, while at the same time securing to all its members that liberty and variety of development which in the case of America had only been fully secured at the cost of disruption.

V

EUROPE AND THE NON-EUROPEAN WORLD 1815-1878

When the European peoples settled down, in 1815, after the long wars of the French Revolution, they found themselves faced by many problems, but there were few Europeans who would have included among these problems the extension of Western civilisation over the as yet unsubjugated portions of the world. Men's hearts were set upon the organisation of permanent peace: that seemed the greatest of all questions, and, for a time, it appeared to have obtained a satisfactory solution with the organisation of the great League of Peace of 1815. But the peace was to be short-lived, because it was threatened by the emergence of a number of other problems of great complexity. First among these stood the problem of nationality: the increasingly clamorous demand of divided or subject peoples for unity and freedom. Alongside of this arose the sister-problem of liberalism: the demand raised from all sides, among peoples who had never known political liberty, for the institutions of self-government which had been proved practicable by the British peoples, and turned into the object of a fervent belief by the preachings of the French. These two causes were to plunge Europe into many wars, and to vex and divide the peoples of every European country, throughout the period 1815-78. And to add to the complexity, there was growing in intensity during all these years the problem of Industrialism—the transformation of the very bases of life in all civilised communities, and the consequent development of wholly new, and terribly difficult, social issues. Preoccupied with all these questions, the statesmen and the peoples of most European states had no attention to spare for the non-European world. They neglected it all the more readily because the events of the preceding period seemed to demonstrate that colonial empires were not worth the cost and labour necessary for their attainment, since they seemed doomed to fall asunder as soon as they began to be valuable.

Yet the period 1815-78 was to see an extension of European civilisation in the non-European world more remarkable than that of any previous age. The main part in this extension was played by Britain, who found herself left free, without serious rivalry in any part of the globe, to expand and develop the extraordinary empire which she possessed in 1815, and to deal with the bewildering problems which it presented. So marked was the British predominance in colonial activity during this age that it has been called the age of British monopoly, and so far as trans-oceanic activities were concerned, this phrase very nearly represents the truth. But there were other developments of the period almost as remarkable as the growth and reorganisation of the British Empire; and it will be convenient to survey these in the first instance before turning to the British achievement.

The place of honour, as always in any great story of European civilisation, belongs to France. Undeterred by the loss of her earlier empire, and unexhausted by the strain of the great ordeal through which she had just passed, France began in these years the creation of her second colonial empire, which was to be in many ways more splendid than the first. Within fifteen years of the fall of Napoleon, the French flag was flying in Algiers.

The northern coast of Africa, from the Gulf of Syrtis to the Atlantic, which has been in modern times divided into the three districts of Tunis, Algeria, and Morocco, forms essentially a single region, whose character is determined by the numerous chains of the Atlas Mountains. This region, shut off from the rest of Africa not only by the Atlas but by the most impassable of all geographical barriers, the great Sahara desert, really belongs to Europe rather than to the continent of which it forms a part. Its fertile valleys were once the homes of brilliant civilisations: they were the seat of the Carthaginian Empire, and at a later date they constituted one of the richest and most civilised provinces of the Roman Empire. Their civilisation was wrecked by that barbarous German tribe, the Vandals, in the fifth century. It received only a partial and temporary revival after the Mahomedan conquest at the end of the seventh century, and since that date this once happy region has gradually lapsed into barbarism. During the modern age it was chiefly known as the home of ruthless and destructive pirates, whose chief headquarters were at Algiers, and who owned a merely nominal allegiance to the Sultan of Turkey. Ever since the time of Khair-ed-din Barbarossa, in the early sixteenth century, the powers of Europe have striven in vain to keep the Barbary corsairs in check. Charles V., Philip II., Louis XIV. attacked them with only temporary success: they continued to terrorise the trade of the Mediterranean, to seize trading-ships, to pillage the shores of Spain and Italy, and to carry off thousands of Christians into a cruel slavery; Robinson Crusoe, it may be recalled, was one of their victims. The powers at Vienna endeavoured to concert action against them in 1815. They were attacked by a British fleet in 1816, and by a combined British and French fleet in 1819. But all such temporary measures were insufficient. The only cure for the ill was that the headquarters of the pirate chiefs should be conquered, and brought under civilised government.

This task France was rather reluctantly drawn into undertaking, as the result of a series of insults offered by the pirates to the French flag between 1827 and 1830. At first the aim of the conquerors was merely to occupy and administer the few ports which formed the chief centres of piracy. But experience showed that this was futile, since it involved endless wars with the unruly clansmen of the interior. Gradually, therefore, the whole of Algeria was systematically conquered and organised. The process took nearly twenty years, and was not completed until 1848. In all the records of European imperialism there has been no conquest more completely justified both by the events which led up to it and by the results which have followed from it. Peace and Law reign throughout a country which had for centuries been given over to anarchy. The wild tribesmen are unlearning the habits of disorder, and being taught to accept the conditions of a civilised life. The great natural resources of the country are being developed as never since the days of Roman rule. No praise can be too high for the work of the French administrators who have achieved these results. And it is worth noting that, alone among the provinces conquered by the European peoples, Algeria has been actually incorporated in the mother-country; it is part of the French Republic, and its elected representatives sit in the French Parliament.

In the nature of things the conquest of Algeria could not stand alone. Algeria is separated by merely artificial lines from Tunis on the east and Morocco on the west, where the old conditions of anarchy still survived; and the establishment of order and peace in the middle area of this single natural region was difficult, so long as the areas on either side remained in disorder and war. In 1844 France found it necessary to make war upon Morocco because of the support which it had afforded to a rebellious Algerian chief, and this episode illustrated the close connection of the two regions. But the troops were withdrawn as soon as the immediate purpose was served. France had not yet begun to think of extending her dominion over the areas to the east and west of Algeria. That was to be the work of the next period.

Further south in Africa, France retained, as a relic of her older empire, a few posts on the coast of West Africa, notably Senegal. From these her intrepid explorers and traders began to extend their influence, and the dream of a great French empire in Northern Africa began to attract French minds. But the realisation of this dream also belongs to the next period. In the Far East, too, this was a period of beginnings. Ever since 1787 — before the Revolution — the French had possessed a foothold on the coast of Annam, from which French missionaries carried on their labours among the peoples of Indo-China. Maltreatment of these missionaries led to a war with Annam in 1858, and in 1862 the extreme south of the Annamese Empire — the province of Cochin-China — was ceded to France. Lastly, the French obtained a foothold in the Pacific, by the annexation of Tahiti and the Marquesas Islands in 1842, and of New Caledonia in 1855. But in 1878 the French dominions in the non-European world were, apart from Algeria, of slight importance. They were quite insignificant in comparison with the far-spreading realms of her ancient rival, Britain.

On a much greater scale than the expansion of France was the expansion of the already vast Russian Empire during this period. The history of Russia in the nineteenth century is made up of a series of alternations between a regime of comparative liberalism, when the interest of government and people was chiefly turned towards the west, and a regime of reaction, when the government endeavoured to pursue what was called a 'national' or purely Russian policy, and to exclude all Western influences. During these long intervals of reaction, attention was turned eastward; and it was in the reactionary periods, mainly, that the Russian power was rapidly extended in three directions — over the Caucasus, over Central Asia, and in the Far East.

Before this advance, the huge Russian Empire had been (everywhere except on the west, in the region of Poland) marked off by very clearly defined barriers. The Caucasus presented a formidable obstacle between Russia and the Turkish and Persian Empires; the deserts of Central Asia separated her from the Moslem peoples of Khiva, Bokhara and Turkestan; the huge range of the Altai Mountains and the desert of Gobi cut off her thinly peopled province of Eastern Siberia from the Chinese Empire; while in the remote East her shores verged upon ice-bound and inhospitable seas. Hers was thus an extraordinarily isolated and self-contained empire, except on the side of Europe; and even on the side of Europe she was more inaccessible than any other state, being all but land-locked, and divided from Central Europe by a belt of forests and marshes.

The part she had played in the Napoleonic Wars, and in the events which followed them, had brought her more fully into contact with Europe than she had ever been before. The acquisition of Poland and Finland, which she obtained by the treaties of 1815, had increased this contact, for both of these states were much influenced by Western ideas. Russia had promised that their distinct national existence, and their national institutions, should be preserved; and this seemed to suggest that the Russian Empire might develop into a partnership of nations of varying types, not altogether unlike the form into which the British Empire was developing. But this conception had no attraction for the Russian mind, or at any rate for the Russian government; and the reactionary or pure-Russian school, which strove to exclude all alien influences, was inevitably hostile to it. Hence the period of reaction, and of eastward conquest, saw also the denial of the promises made in 1815. Poland preserved her distinct national organisation, in any full degree, only for fifteen years; even in the faintest degree, it was preserved for less than fifty years. Finland was allowed a longer grace, but only, perhaps, because she was isolated and had but a small population: her turn for 'Russification' was to come in due course. The exclusion of Western influence, the segregation of Russia from the rest of the world, and the repudiation of liberty and of varieties of type thus form the main features of the reactionary periods which filled the greater part of this age; and the activity of Russia in eastward expansion was in part intended to forward this policy, by diverting the attention of the Russian people from the west towards the east, and by substituting the pride of dominion for the desire for liberty. Hence imperialism came to be identified, for the Russian people, with the denial of liberty.

But it is a very striking fact that each of the three main lines of territorial advance followed by Russia in Asia during this period led her to overstep the natural barriers which had made her an isolated and self-dependent empire, brought her into relation with other civilisations, and compelled her to play her part as one of the factors in world-politics.

Russia had begun the conquest of the wild Caucasus region as early as 1802; after a long series of wars, she completed it by the acquisition of the region of Kars in 1878. The mastery of the Caucasus brought her into immediate relation with the Armenian province of the Turkish Empire, which she henceforward threatened from the east as well as from the west. It brought her into contact also with the Persian Empire, over whose policy, from 1835 onwards, she wielded a growing influence, to the perturbation of Britain. And besides bringing her into far closer relations with the two greatest Mahomedan powers, it gave her a considerable number of Mahomedan subjects, since some of the Caucasus tribes belonged to that faith.

Again, the conquest of Central Asia led her to overstep the barrier of the Kirghiz deserts. The wandering Kirghiz and Turkoman tribes of this barren region lived largely upon the pillage of caravans, and upon raids into neighbouring countries; they disposed of their spoil (which often included Russian captives) mainly in the bazars of Bokhara, Khiva, Samarkand and Khokand—Mahomedan Khanates which occupied the more fertile areas in the southern and south-eastern part of the desert region. The attempt to control the Turkoman raiders brought Russia into conflict with these outposts of Islam. Almost the whole of this region was conquered in a long series of campaigns between 1848 and 1876. These conquests (which covered an area 1200 miles from east to west and 600 miles from north to south) made Russia a great Mahomedan power. They also brought her into direct contact with Afghanistan. Russian agents were at work in Afghanistan from 1838 onwards. The shadow of her vast power, looming over Persia and the Persian Gulf on the one hand, and over the mountain frontiers of India on the other, naturally appeared highly menacing to Britain. It was the direct cause of the advance of the British power from the Indus over North-Western India, until it could rest upon the natural frontier of the mountains—an advance which took place mainly during the years 1839-49. And it formed the chief source of the undying suspicion of Russia which was the dominant note of British foreign policy throughout the period.

Another feature of these conquests was that, taken in conjunction with the French conquest of Algeria and the British conquest of India, they constituted the first serious impact of European civilisation upon the vast realm of Islam. Until now the regions of the Middle East which had been subjugated by the followers of Mahomed had repelled every attack of the West. More definite in its creed, and more exacting in its demands upon the allegiance of its adherents, than any other religion, Mahomedanism had for more than a thousand years been able to resist with extraordinary success the influence of other civilisations; and it had been, from the time of the Crusades onwards, the most formidable opponent of the civilisation of the West. Under the rule of the Turk the Mahomedan world had become stagnant and sterile, and it had shut out not merely the direct control of the West (which would have been legitimate enough), but the influence of Western ideas. All the innumerable schemes of reform which were based upon the retention of the old regime in the Turkish Empire have hopelessly broken down; and the only chance for an awakening in these lands of ancient civilisation seemed to depend upon the breakdown of the old system under the impact of Western imperialism or insurgent nationalism. It has only been during the nineteenth century, as a result of Russian, French, and British imperialism, that the resisting power of Islam has begun to give way to the influence of Europe.

The third line of Russian advance was on the Pacific coast, where in the years 1858 and 1860 Russia obtained from China the Amur province, with the valuable harbour of Vladivostok. It was an almost empty land, but its acquisition made Russia a Pacific power, and brought her into very close neighbourhood with China, into whose reserved markets, at the same period, the maritime powers of the West were forcing an entrance. At the same time Russian relations with Japan, which were to have such pregnant consequences, were beginning: in 1875 the Japanese were forced to cede the southern half of the island of Sakhalin, and perhaps we may date from this year the suspicion of Russia which dominated Japanese policy for a long time to come.

Thus, while in Europe Russia was trying to shut herself off from contact with the world, her advances in Asia had brought her at three points into the full stream of world-politics. Her vast empire, though for the most part very thinly peopled, formed beyond all comparison the greatest continuous area ever brought under a single rule, since it amounted to between eight and nine million square miles; and when the next age, the age of rivalry for world-power, began, this colossal fabric of power haunted and dominated the imaginations of men.

A demonstration of the growing power of Western civilisation, even more impressive than the expansion of the Russian Empire, was afforded during these years by the opening to Western influence of the ancient, pot-bound empires of the Far East, China and Japan. The opening of China began with the Anglo-Chinese War of 1840, which led to the acquisition of Hong-Kong and the opening of a group of treaty ports to European trade. It was carried further by the combined Franco-British war of 1857-58, which was ended by a treaty permitting the free access of European travellers, traders, and missionaries to the interior, and providing for the permanent residence of ambassadors of the signatory powers at the court of Pekin. All the European states rushed to share these privileges, and the Westernising of China had begun. It did not take place rapidly or completely, and it was accompanied by grave disturbances, notably the Taiping rebellion, which was only suppressed by the aid of the British General Gordon, in command of a Chinese army. But though the process was slow, it was fully at work by 1878. The external trade of China, nearly all in European hands, had assumed great proportions. The missionaries and schoolmasters of Europe and America were busily at work in the most populous provinces. Shanghai had become a European city, and one of the great trade-centres of the world. In a lame and incompetent way the Chinese government was attempting to organise its army on the European model, and to create a navy after the European style. Steamboats were plying on the Yang-tse-kiang, and the first few miles of railway were open. Chinese students were beginning to resort to the universities and schools of the West; and although the conservatism of the Chinese mind was very slow to make the plunge, it was already plain that this vast hive of patient, clever, and industrious men was bound to enter the orbit of Western civilisation.

Meanwhile, after a longer and stiffer resistance, Japan had made up her mind to a great change with amazing suddenness and completeness. There had been some preliminary relations with the Western peoples, beginning with the visits of the American Commodore Perry in 1853 and 1854, and a few ports had been opened to European trade. But then came a sudden, violent reaction (1862). The British embassy was attacked; a number of British subjects were murdered; a mixed fleet of British, French, Dutch, and American ships proved the power of Western arms, and Japan began to awaken to the necessity of adopting, in self-defence, the methods of these intrusive foreigners. The story of the internal revolution in Japan, which began in

1866, cannot be told here; enough that it led to the most astounding change in history. Emerging from her age-long isolation and from her contentment with her ancient, unchanging modes of life, Japan realised that the future lay with the restless and progressive civilisation of the West; and with a national resolve to which there is no sort of parallel or analogy in history, decided that she must not wait to be brought under subjection, but must adopt the new methods and ideas for herself, if possible without shedding too much of her ancient traditions. By a deliberate exercise of the will and an extraordinary effort of organisation, she became industrial without ceasing to be artistic; she adopted parliamentary institutions without abandoning her religious veneration for the person of the Mikado; she borrowed the military methods of the West without losing the chivalrous and fatalist devotion of her warrior-caste; and devised a Western educational system without disturbing the deep orientalism of her mind. It was a transformation almost terrifying, and to any Western quite bewildering, in its deliberation, rapidity, and completeness. Europe long remained unconvinced of its reality. But in 1878 the work was, in its essentials, already achieved, and the one state of non-European origin which has been able calmly to choose what she would accept and what she would reject among the systems and methods of the West, stood ready to play an equal part with the European nations in the later stages of the long imperial struggle.

One last sphere of activity remains to be surveyed before we turn to consider the development of the new British Empire: the expansion of the independent states which had arisen on the ruins of the first colonial empires in the New World. Of the Spanish and Portuguese states of Central and South America it is not necessary to say much. They had established their independence between 1815 and 1825. But the unhappy traditions of the long Spanish ascendancy had rendered them incapable of using freedom well, and Central and South America became the scene of ceaseless and futile revolutions. The influence of the American Monroe Doctrine forbade, perhaps fortunately, the intervention of any of the European states to put an end to this confusion, and America herself made no serious attempt to restrain it. It was not until the later years of our period that any large stream of immigration began to flow into these lands from other European countries than Spain and Portugal, and that their vast natural resources began to be developed by the energy and capital of Europe. But by 1878 the more fertile of these states, Argentina, Brazil, and Chili, were being enriched by these means, were becoming highly important elements in the trade-system of the world, and were consequently beginning to achieve a more stable and settled civilisation. In some regards this work (though it belongs mainly to the period after 1878) constitutes one of the happiest results of the extra-European activities of the

European peoples during the nineteenth century. It was carried on, in the main, not by governments or under government encouragement, but by the private enterprises of merchants and capitalists; and while a very large part in these enterprises was played by British and American traders and settlers, one of the most notable features of the growth of South America was that it gave play to some of the European peoples, notably the Germans and the Italians, whose part in the political division of the world was relatively small.

Far more impressive was the almost miraculous expansion which came to the United States during this period. When the United States started upon their career as an independent nation in 1782, their territory was limited to the lands east of the Mississippi, excluding Florida, which was still retained by Spain. Only the eastern margin of this area was at all fully settled; and the population numbered at most 2,000,000, predominantly of British blood. In 1803, by a treaty with Napoleon, the French colony of Louisiana, with vast and ill-defined claims to the territory west of the Mississippi, was purchased from France. Meanwhile the stream of immigrants from the eastern states, and in a less degree from Europe, was pouring over the Alleghany Mountains and occupying the great central plain; and by 1815 the population had risen to almost 9,000,000, still mainly of British stock, though it also included substantial French and German elements, as well as large numbers of negro slaves. In 1819 Florida was acquired by purchase from Spain. In 1845-48 a revolution in Texas (then part of Mexico), followed by two Mexican wars, led to the annexation of a vast area extending from the Gulf of Mexico to the Pacific coast, including the paradise of California; while treaties with Britain in 1818 and 1846 determined the northern boundary of the States, and secured their control over the regions of Washington and Oregon.

Thus the imperialist spirit was working as irresistibly in the democratic communities of the New World as in the monarchies of Europe. Not content with the possession of vast and almost unpeopled areas, they had spread their dominion from ocean to ocean, and built up an empire less extensive indeed than that of Russia, but even more compact, far richer in resources, and far better suited to be the home of a highly civilised people. Into this enormous area there began to pour a mighty flood of immigration from Europe, as soon as the Napoleonic wars were over. By 1878 the population of the States had risen to about 50,000,000, and was greater than that of any European state save Russia. A new world-state of the first rank had arisen. It was made up of contributions from all the European peoples. Those of British stock, especially the Irish, still predominated throughout this period, but the Germans and the Scandinavians were becoming increasingly numerous, and the Italians, Greeks, Poles, Czechs, Russian Jews, and other stocks were beginning to form very substantial elements. It was a melting-pot of races, which had to be somehow welded into a nation by the moulding-power of the traditions implanted by the earlier British settlers. It may fairly be said that no community has ever had imposed upon it a more difficult task than the task imposed by Fate upon the American people of creating a national unity out of this heterogeneous material. The great experiment was, during this period, singularly successful. The strength of the national sentiment and of the tradition of freedom was very powerfully exhibited in the strain of the great Civil War (1861-65) which maintained at a great cost the threatened unity of the republic, and brought about the emancipation of the negro slaves. And the Civil War produced in Abraham Lincoln a national hero, and an exponent of the national character and ideals, worthy to be set beside Washington. The America of Lincoln manifestly stood for Liberty and Justice, the fundamental ideals of Western civilisation.

But in this great moulding tradition of freedom there was one dubious and narrowing element. Accustomed to regard herself as having achieved liberty by shaking off her connection with the Old World, America was tempted to think of this liberty as something peculiar to herself, something which the 'effete monarchies' of the Old World did not, and could not, fully understand or share, something which exempted her from responsibility for the non-American world, and from the duty of aiding and defending liberty beyond her own limits. In the abounding prosperity of this fortunate land, liberty was apt to be too readily identified merely with the opportunity of securing material prosperity, and the love of liberty was apt to become, what indeed it too often is everywhere, a purely self-regarding emotion. The distance of the republic from Europe and its controversies, its economic self-sufficiency, its apparent security against all attack, fostered and strengthened this feeling. While the peoples of the Old World strove with agony and travail towards freedom and justice, or wrestled with the task of sharing their own civilisation with the backward races of the globe, the echo of their strivings penetrated but faintly into the mind of America, like the noises of the street dimly heard through the shuttered windows of a warmed and lighted room. To the citizens of the Middle West and the Far West, especially, busy as they were with the development of vast untapped resources, the affairs of the outer world necessarily appeared remote and insignificant. Even their newspapers told them little about these far-off events. Naturally it appeared that the function of the republic in the progress of the world was to till its own garden, and to afford a haven of refuge to the oppressed and impoverished who poured in from all lands; and this idea was strengthened by the great number of immigrants who were driven to the New World by the failure of the successive European revolutions of the nineteenth century, and by the oppressive tyranny of the Habsburg monarchy and the Russian despots.

This attitude of aloofness from, and contempt, or, at the best, indifference, to the Old World was further encouraged by the traditional treatment of American history. The outstanding event of that story was, of course, the breach with Britain, with which the independent existence of the Republic began, and which constituted also almost its only direct contact with the politics of the Old World. The view of this conflict which was driven into the national mind by the school-books, by the annual celebrations of the Fourth of July, and by incessant newspaper writing, represented the great quarrel not as a dispute in a family of free communities, in which a new and very difficult problem was raised, and in which there were faults on both sides, but as one in which all the right was on one side, as a heroic resistance of free men against malevolent tyranny. This view has been profoundly modified by the work of American historians, whose researches during the last generation have transformed the treatment of the American Revolution. To-day the old one-sided view finds expression, in books of serious pretensions, only in England; and it is to American scholars that we must have recourse for a more scientific and impartial treatment. But the new and saner view has scarcely yet made its way into the school-books and the newspapers. If Britain, the mother of political liberty in the modern world, the land from which these freemen had inherited their own liberties and the spirit which made them insist upon their enlargement, was made to appear a tyrant power, how could it be expected that the mass of Americans, unversed in world-politics, should follow with sympathy the progress of liberty beyond the limits of their own republic? It was in the light of this traditional attitude that the bulk of Americans regarded not only the wars and controversies of Europe, but the vast process of European expansion. All these things did not appear to concern them; they seemed to be caused by motives and ideas which the great republic had outgrown, though, as we have already seen, and shall see again, the republic had by no means outgrown them. The strength of this traditional attitude, fostered as it was by every circumstance, naturally made the bulk of the American people slow to realise, when the great challenge of Germany was forced upon the world, that the problems of world-politics were as vitally important for them as for all other peoples, and that no free nation could afford to be indifferent to the fate of liberty upon the earth.

At one moment, indeed, almost at the beginning of the period, it appeared as if this narrow outlook was about to be abandoned. The League of Peace of the great European powers of 1815[6] had, by 1822, developed into a league of despots for the suppression of revolutionary tendencies. They had intervened to crush revolutionary outbreaks in Naples and Piedmont; they had authorised France to enter Spain in order to destroy the democratic system which had been set up in that country in 1820. Britain alone protested against these interventions, claiming that every state ought to be left free to fix its own form of government; and in 1822 Canning had practically withdrawn from the League of Peace, because it was being turned into an engine of oppression. It was notorious that, Spain once subjugated, the monarchs desired to go on to the reconquest of the revolting Spanish colonies in South America. Britain could not undertake a war on the Continent against all the Continental powers combined, but she could prevent their intervention in America, and Canning made it plain that the British fleet would forbid any such action. To strengthen his hands, he suggested to the American ambassador that the United States might take common action in this sense. The result was the famous message of President Monroe to Congress in December 1823, which declared that the United States accepted the doctrine of non-intervention, and that they would resist any attempt on the part of the European monarchs to establish their reactionary system in the New World.

[6] See "Nationalism and Internationalism".

In effect this was a declaration of support for Britain. It was so regarded by Monroe's most influential adviser, Thomas Jefferson. 'Great Britain,' he wrote, 'is the nation which can do us the most harm of any one, or all, on earth, and with her on our side we need not fear the whole world. With her, then, we should the most sedulously cherish a cordial friendship; and nothing would tend more to knit our affection than to be fighting once more side by side hi the same cause.' To be fighting side by side with Britain in the same cause — the cause of the secure establishment of freedom in the world — this seemed to the Democrat Jefferson an object worth aiming at; and the promise of this seemed to be the main recommendation of the Monroe Doctrine. It was intended as an alliance for the defence of freedom, not as a proclamation of aloofness; and thus America seemed to be taking her natural place as one of the powers concerned to strengthen law and liberty, not only within her own borders, but throughout the world.

The Monroe Doctrine was rapidly accepted as expressing the fundamental principle of American foreign policy. But under the influence of the powerful tradition which we have attempted to analyse, its significance was gradually changed; and instead of being interpreted as a proclamation that the great republic could not be indifferent to the fate of liberty, and would co-operate to defend it from attack in all cases where such co-operation was reasonably practicable, it came to be interpreted by average public opinion as meaning that America had no concern with the politics of the Old World, and that the states of the Old World must not be allowed to meddle in any of the affairs of either American continent. The world of civilisation was to be divided into water-tight compartments; as if it were not indissolubly one. Yet even in this rather narrow form, the Monroe doctrine has on the whole been productive of good; it has helped to save South America from becoming one of the fields of rivalry of the European powers.

But it may be doubted whether the mere enunciation of the doctrine, even in this precise and definite form, has of itself been sufficient to secure this end. There is good reason to believe that the doctrine would not have been safe from challenge if it had not been safeguarded by the supremacy of the British Fleet. For throughout the last half-century all the world has known that any defiance of this doctrine, and any attack upon America, would bring Britain into the field. During all this period one of the factors of world-politics has been the existence of an informal and one-sided alliance between Britain and America. The alliance has been informal, because it has not rested upon any treaty or even upon any definite understanding. It has been one-sided, because while average opinion in America has been distrustful of Britain, has been apt to put unfavourable constructions upon British policy, and has generally failed to appreciate the value and significance of the work which Britain has done in the outer world, Britain, on the other hand, has always known that America stood for justice and freedom; and therefore, however difficult the relations between the two powers might occasionally become, Britain has steadfastly refused to consider the possibility of a breach with America, and with rare exceptions has steadily given her support to American policy. The action of the British squadron off the Philippines in 1898, in quietly interposing itself between the threatening German guns and the American Fleet, has, in fact, been broadly typical of the British attitude. This factor has not only helped to preserve the Monroe Doctrine from challenge, it has indirectly contributed to deepen the American conviction that it was possible, even in the changed conditions of the modern world, to maintain a complete isolation from the political controversies of the powers.

During the period 1815-1878, then, while the greater part of Europe was still indifferent to extra-European affairs, America had developed into a vast state wherein freedom and law were enthroned, a huge melting-pot wherein diverse peoples were being gradually unified and turned into a new nation under the moulding power of a great tradition of liberty. But her geographical position, and certain elements in her tradition, had hitherto led her to abstain from, and even to repudiate, that great part in the shaping of the common destinies of civilisation to which she was manifestly called by her wealth, her numbers, her freedom, and her share in the traditions of all the European peoples. In the nature of things, whatever some Americans might think, this voluntary isolation could not continue for ever. It was to be brought to an end by the fevered developments of the next era, and by the great challenge to the liberties of the world in which it culminated.

VI

THE TRANSFORMATION OF THE BRITISH EMPIRE, 1815-1878

Mighty as had been the achievements of other lands which have been surveyed in the last section, the main part in the expansion of European civilisation over the world during the first three-quarters of the nineteenth century was played by Britain. For she was engaged in opening out new continents and sub-continents; and she was giving an altogether new significance to the word 'Empire.' Above all, she was half-blindly laying the foundations of a system whereby freedom and the enriching sense of national unity might be realised at once in the new and vacant lands of the earth, and among its oldest civilised peoples; she was feeling her way towards a mode of linking diverse and free states in a common brotherhood of peace and mutual respect. There is no section of the history of European imperialism more interesting than the story of the growth and organisation of the heterogeneous and disparate empire with which Britain entered upon the new age.

This development appeared, on the surface, to be quite haphazard, and to be governed by no clearly grasped theories or policy. It is indeed true that at all times British policy has not been governed by theory, but by the moulding force of a tradition of ordered freedom. The period produced in Britain no imperialist statesman of the first rank, nor did imperial questions play a leading part in the deliberations of parliament. In fact, the growth of the British Empire and its organisation were alike spontaneous and unsystematic; their only guide (but it proved to be a good guide) was the spirit of self-government, existing in every scattered section of the people; and the part played by the colonists themselves, and by the administrative officers in India and elsewhere, was throughout more important than the part played by colonial secretaries, East Indian directors, parliamentarians and publicists at home. For that reason the story is not easily handled in a broad and simple way.

Enjoying almost a monopoly of oversea activity, Britain was free, in most parts of the world, to expand her dominions as she thought fit. Her statesmen, however, were far from desiring further expansion: they rightly felt that the responsibilities already assumed were great enough to tax the resources of any state, however rich and populous. But, try as they would, they could not prevent the inevitable process of expansion. Several causes contributed to produce this result. Perhaps the most important was the unexampled growth of British trade, which during these years dominated the whole world; and the flag is apt to follow trade. A second cause was the pressure of economic distress and the extraordinarily rapid increase of population at home, leading to wholesale emigration; in the early years of the century an extravagantly severe penal code, which inflicted the penalty of death, commonly commuted into transportation, for an incredible number of offences, gave an artificial impetus to this movement. The restless and adventurous spirit of the settlers in huge and unexplored new countries contributed another motive for expansion. And in some cases, notably in India, political necessity seemed to demand annexations. Over a movement thus stimulated, the home authorities found themselves, with the best will in the world, unable to exercise any effective restraint; and the already colossal British Empire continued to grow. It is no doubt to be regretted that other European nations were not able during this period to take part in the development of the non-European world in a more direct way than by sending emigrants to America or the British lands. But it is quite certain that the growth of British territory is not to be attributed in any degree to the deliberate policy, or to the greed, of the home government, which did everything in its power to check it.

In India the Russian menace seemed to necessitate the adoption of a policy towards the independent states of the North-West which brought an extension of the frontier, between 1839 and 1849, to the great mountain ranges which form the natural boundary of India in this direction; while a succession of intolerable and quite unprovoked aggressions by the Burmese led to a series of wars which resulted in the annexation of very great territories in the east and north-east: Assam, Aracan, and Tenasserim hi 1825; Pegu and Rangoon in 1853; finally, in 1885-86, the whole remainder of the Burmese Empire. In North America settlers found their way across the Rocky Mountains or over the Isthmus of Panama into the region of British Columbia, which was given a distinct colonial organisation in 1858; and the colonisation of the Red River Settlement, 1811-18, which became hi 1870 the province of Manitoba, began the development of the great central plain. In South Africa frontier wars with the Kaffirs, and the restless movements of Boer trekkers, brought about an expansion of the limits of Cape Colony, the annexation of Natal, and the temporary annexation of the Orange River Settlement and the Transvaal; but all these additions were most reluctantly accepted; the Orange River Settlement and the Transvaal soon had their independence restored, though the former, at any rate, accepted it unwillingly. In Australia, drafts of new settlers planting themselves at new points led to the organisation of six distinct colonies between 1825 and 1859; and this implied the definite annexation of the whole continent. New Zealand was annexed in 1839, but only because British traders had already established themselves in the islands, were in unhappy relations with the natives, and had to be brought under control.

But it was not the territorial expansion of the British Empire which gave significance to this period in its history, but, in a far higher degree, the new principles of government which were developed during its course. The new colonial policy which gradually shaped itself during this age was so complete a departure from every precedent of the past, and represented so remarkable an experiment in imperial government, that its sources deserve a careful analysis. It was brought into being by a number of distinct factors and currents of opinion which were at work both in Britain and in the colonies.

In the first place, there existed in Britain, as in other European countries, a large body of opinion which held that all colonies were sure to demand and obtain their independence as soon as they became strong enough to desire it; that as independent states they could be quite as profitable to the mother-country as they could ever be while they remained attached to her, more especially if the parting took place without bitterness; and that the wisest policy for Britain to pursue was therefore to facilitate their development, to place no barrier in the way of the increase of their self-government, and to enable them at the earliest moment to start as free nations on their own account. This was not, indeed, the universal, nor perhaps even the preponderant, attitude in regard to the colonies in the middle of the nineteenth century. But it was pretty common. It appeared in the most unexpected quarters, as when Disraeli said that the colonies were 'millstones about our necks,' or as when The Times advocated in a leading article the cession of Canada to the United States, on the ground that annexation to the great Republic was the inevitable destiny of that colony, and that it was much better that it should be carried out in a peaceable and friendly way than after a conflict. It is difficult to-day to realise that men could ever have entertained such opinions. But they were widely held; and it must at least be obvious that the prevalence of these views is quite inconsistent with the idea that Britain was deliberately following a policy of expansion and annexation in this age. Men who held these opinions (and they were to be found in every party) regarded with resentment and alarm every addition to what seemed to them the useless burdens assumed by the nation, and required to be satisfied that every new annexation of territory was not merely justifiable, but inevitable.

A second factor which contributed to the change of attitude towards the colonies was the growing influence of a new school of economic thought, the school of Adam Smith, Ricardo, and Malthus. Their ideas had begun to affect national policy as early as the twenties, when Huskisson took the first steps on the way to free trade. In the thirties the bulk of the trading and industrial classes had become converts to these ideas, which won their definite victories in the budgets of Sir Robert Peel, 1843-46, and in those of his disciple Gladstone. The essence of this doctrine, as it affected colonial policy, was that the regulation of trade by government, which had been the main object of the old colonial policy, brought no advantages, but only checked its free development. And for a country in the position which Britain then occupied, this was undeniably true; so overwhelming was her preponderance in world-trade that every current seemed to set in her direction, and the removal of artificial barriers, originally designed to train the current towards her shores, allowed it to follow its natural course. The only considerable opposition to this body of economic doctrine came from those who desired to protect British agriculture; but this motive had (at this period) no bearing upon colonial trade. The triumph of the doctrine of free trade meant that the principal motive which had earlier led to restrictions upon the self-government of the colonies — the desire to secure commercial advantages for the mother-country — was no longer operative. The central idea of the old colonial system was destroyed by the disciples of Adam Smith; and there no longer remained any apparent reason why the mother-country should desire to control the fiscal policy of the colonies. An even more important result of the adoption of this new economic doctrine was that it destroyed every motive which would lead the British government to endeavour to secure for British traders a monopoly of the traffic with British possessions. Henceforth all territories administered under the direct control of the home government were thrown open as freely to the merchants of other countries as to those of Britain herself. The part which Britain now undertook in the undeveloped regions of her empire (except in so far as they were controlled by fully self-governing colonies) was simply that of maintaining peace and law; and in these regions she adopted an attitude which may fairly be described as the attitude, not of a monopolist, but of a trustee for civilisation. It was this policy which explains the small degree of jealousy with which the rapid expansion of her territory was regarded by the rest of the civilised world. If the same policy had been followed, not necessarily at home, but in their colonial possessions, by all the colonising powers, the motives for colonial rivalry would have been materially diminished, and the claims of various states to colonial territories, when the period of rivalry began, would have been far more easily adjusted.

These were negative forces, leading merely to the abandonment of the older colonial theories. But there were also positive and constructive forces at work. First among them may be noted a new body of definite theory as to the function which colonies ought to play in the general economy of the civilised world. It was held to be their function not (as in the older theory) to afford lucrative opportunities for trade to the mother-country: so far as trade was concerned it seemed to matter little whether a country was a colony or an independent state. But the main object of colonisation was, on this view, the systematic draining-off of the surplus population of the older lands. This, it was felt, could not safely be left to the operation of mere chance; and one of the great advantages of colonial possessions was that they enabled the country which controlled them to deal in a scientific way with its surplus population, and to prevent the reproduction of unhealthy conditions in the new communities, which was apt to result if emigrants were allowed to drift aimlessly wheresoever chance took them, and received no guidance as to the proper modes of establishing themselves in their new homes. The great apostle of this body of colonial theory was Edward Gibbon Wakefield; and his book, A View of the Art of Colonisation (1847), deserves to be noted as one of the classics of the history of imperialism. He did not confine himself to theory, but was tireless in organising practical experiments. They were carried out, in a curious revival of the methods of the seventeenth century, by means of a series of colonising companies which Wakefield promoted. The settlement of South Australia, the first considerable settlement in the North Island of New Zealand, and the two admirably designed and executed settlements of Canterbury and Otago in the South Island of New Zealand, were all examples of his methods: with the exception of the North Island settlement, they were all very successful. Nor were these the only instances of organised and assisted emigration. In 1820 a substantial settlement, financed by government, was made in the eastern part of Cape Colony, in the region of Grahamstown and Port Elizabeth, and this brought the first considerable body of British inhabitants into South Africa, hitherto almost exclusively Dutch. An unsuccessful plantation at Swan River in West Australia may also be noted. Systematic and scientific colonisation was thus being studied in Britain during this period as never before. In the view of its advocates Britain was the trustee of civilisation for the administration of the most valuable unpeopled regions of the earth, and it was her duty to see that they were skilfully utilised. So high a degree of success attended some of their efforts that it is impossible not to regret that they were not carried further. But they depended upon Crown control of undeveloped lands. With the growth of full self-government in the colonies the exercise of these Crown functions was transferred from the ministry and parliament of Britain to the ministries and parliaments of the colonies; and this transference put an end to the possibility of a centralised organisation and direction of emigration.

A second constructive factor very potently at work during this age was the humanitarian spirit, which had become a powerful factor in British life during the late eighteenth and early nineteenth centuries. It had received perhaps its most practical expression in the abolition of the slave-trade in 1806, and the campaign against the slave-trade in the rest of the world became an important object of British policy from that time onwards. Having abolished the slave-trade, the humanitarians proceeded to advocate the complete abolition of negro slavery throughout the British Empire. They won their victory in 1833, when the British parliament declared slavery illegal throughout the Empire, and voted 20,000,000 pounds—at a time when British finance was still suffering from the burdens of the Napoleonic War—to purchase from their masters the freedom of all the slaves then existing in the Empire. It was a noble deed, but it was perhaps carried out a little too suddenly, and it led to grave difficulties, especially in the West Indies, whose prosperity was seriously impaired, and in South Africa, where it brought about acute friction with the slave-owning Boer farmers. But it gave evidence of the adoption of a new attitude towards the backward races, hitherto mercilessly exploited by all the imperialist powers. One expression of this attitude had already been afforded by the organisation (1787) of the colony of Sierra Leone, on the West African coast, as a place of refuge for freed slaves desiring to return to the land of their fathers.

It was principally through the activity of missionaries that this new point of view was expressed and cultivated. Organised missionary activity in Britain dates from the end of the eighteenth century, but its range grew with extraordinary rapidity throughout the period. And wherever the missionaries went, they constituted themselves the protectors and advocates of the native races among whom they worked. Often enough they got themselves into bad odour with the European traders and settlers with whom they came in contact. But through their powerful home organisations they exercised very great influence over public opinion and over government policy. The power of 'Exeter Hall,' where the religious bodies and the missionary societies held their meetings in London, was at its height in the middle of the nineteenth century, and politicians could not afford to disregard it, even if they had desired to do so. This influence, supporting the trend of humanitarian opinion, succeeded in establishing it as one of the principles of British imperial policy that it was the duty of the British government to protect the native races against the exploitation of the European settlers, and to guide them gently into a civilised way of life. It is a sound and noble principle, and it may fairly be said that it has been honestly carried out, so far as the powers of the home government rendered possible. No government in the world controls a greater number or variety of subjects belonging to the backward races than the British; no trading nation has had greater opportunities for the oppressive exploitation of defenceless subjects. Yet the grave abuse of these opportunities has been infrequent. There have been in the history of modern British imperialism sporadic instances of injustice, like the forced labour of Kanakas in the Pacific. But there have been no Congo outrages, no Putumayo atrocities, no Pequena slave scandals, no merciless slaughter like that of the Hereros in German South-West Africa.

The principle of the protection of backward peoples has, however, sometimes had an unfortunate influence upon colonial policy; and there was no colony in which it exercised a more unhappy effect than South Africa. Here the Boer farmers still retained towards their native neighbours the attitude which had been characteristic of all the European peoples in the seventeenth and eighteenth centuries: they regarded the negro as a natural inferior, born to servitude. It is not surprising that no love was lost between the Boers and the missionaries, who appeared as the protectors of the negroes, and whose representations turned British opinion violently against the whole Boer community. This was in itself a sufficiently unfortunate result: it lies largely at the base of the prolonged disharmony which divided the two peoples in South Africa. The belief that the Boers could not be trusted to deal fairly with the natives formed, for a long period, the chief reason which urged the British Government to retain their control over the Boers, even when they had trekked away from the Cape (1836) and established themselves beyond the Orange and the Vaal rivers; and the conflict of this motive with the desire to avoid any increase of colonial responsibilities, and with the feeling that if the Boers disliked the British system, they had better be left in freedom to organise themselves in their own way, accounts for the curious vacillation in the policy of the period on this question. At first the trekkers were left to themselves; then the lands which they had occupied were annexed; then their independence was recognised; and finally, when, at the end of the period, they seemed to be causing a dangerous excitement among the Zulus and other native tribes, the Transvaal was once more annexed; with the result that revolt broke out, and the Majuba campaign had to be fought.

Again, tenderness for the natives led to several curious and not very successful experiments in organisation. The annexation of Natal was long delayed because it was held that this area ought to form a native reserve, and fruitless attempts were made to restrict the settlement of Europeans in this empty and fertile land. An attempt was also made to set up a series of native areas under British protection, from which the white settler was excluded. British Kaffraria, Griqualand East and Griqualand West were examples of this policy, which is still represented, not unsuccessfully, by the great protected area of Basutoland. But, on the whole, these experiments in the handling of the native problem in South Africa did more harm than good. They were unsuccessful mainly because South Africa was a white man's country, into which the most vigorous of the native races, those of the Bantu stock (Kaffirs, Zulus, Matabili, etc.), were more recent immigrants than the white men themselves. Owing to their warlike character and rapidly growing numbers they constituted for a long time a very formidable danger; and neither the missionaries nor the home authorities sufficiently recognised these facts.

Perhaps the most unhappy result of this friction over the native question, apart from the alienation of Boer and Briton which it produced, was the fact that it was the principal cause of the long delay in establishing self-governing institutions in South Africa. The home government hesitated to give to the colonists full control over their own affairs, because it distrusted the use which they were likely to make of their powers over the natives; even the normal institutions of all British colonies were not established in Cape Colony till 1854, and in Natal till 1883. But although in this case the new attitude towards the backward races led to some unhappy results, the spirit which inspired it was altogether admirable, and its growing strength accounts in part for the real degree of success which has been achieved by British administrators in the government of regions not suited for the settlement of Europeans in large numbers. Indeed, this spirit has come to be one of the outstanding features of modern British imperialism.

It was not only in the treatment of backward races that the humanitarian spirit made itself felt. It was at work also in the government of the highly developed civilisations of India, where, during this period, British power began to be boldly used to put an end to barbarous or inhumane practices which were supported or tolerated by the religious beliefs or immemorial social usages of India. Such practices as thagi, or meria sacrifices, or female infanticide, or, above all, sati, had been left undisturbed by the earlier rulers of British India, because they feared that interference with them would be resented as an infraction of Indian custom or religion. They were now boldly attacked, and practically abolished, without evil result.

Alongside of this new courage in measures that seemed to be dictated by the moral ideas of the West, there was to be seen growing throughout this period a new temper of respect for Indian civilisation and a desire to study and understand it, and to safeguard its best features. The study of early Indian literature, law, and religious philosophy had indeed been begun in the eighteenth century by Sir William Jones and Nathaniel Halhed, with the ardent encouragement of Warren Hastings. But in this as in other respects Hastings was ahead of the political opinion of his time; the prevalent idea was that the best thing for India would be the introduction, so far as possible, of British methods. This led to the absurdities of the Supreme Court, established in 1773 to administer English law to Indians. It led also to the great blunder of Cornwallis's settlement of the land question in Bengal, which was an attempt to assimilate the Indian land-system to that of England, and resulted in an unhappy weakening of the village communities, the most healthy features of Indian rural life. In the nineteenth century this attitude was replaced by a spirit of respect for Indian traditions and methods of organisation, and by a desire to retain and strengthen their best features. The new attitude was perhaps to be seen at its best in the work of Mountstuart Elphinstone, a great administrator who was also a profound student of Indian history, and a very sympathetic observer and friend of Indian customs and modes of life. But the same spirit was exemplified by the whole of the remarkable generation of statesmen of whom Elphinstone was one. They established the view that it was the duty of the British power to reorganise India, indeed, but to reorganise it on lines in accordance with its own traditions. Above all, the principle was in this generation very definitely established that India, like other great dependencies, must be administered in the interests of its own people, and not in the interests of the ruling race. That seems to us to-day a platitude. It would not have seemed a platitude in the eighteenth century. It would not seem a platitude in modern Germany. And it may safely be said that the enunciation of such a doctrine would have seemed merely absurd in any of the earlier historical empires. In 1833 an official report laid before the British parliament contained these remarkable words: 'It is recognised as an indisputable principle, that the interests of the Native Subjects are to be consulted in preference to those of Europeans, wherever the two come in competition.' In all the records of imperialism it would be hard to find a parallel to this formal statement of policy by the supreme government of a ruling race. When such a statement could be made, it is manifest that the meaning of the word Empire had undergone a remarkable transformation. No one can read the history of British rule in India during this period without feeling that, in spite of occasional lapses, this was its real spirit.

But the most powerful constructive element in the shaping of the new imperial policy of Britain was the strength of the belief in the idea of self-government, as not only morally desirable but practically efficacious, which was to be perceived at work in the political circles of Britain during this age. Self-government had throughout the modern age been a matter of habit and practice with the British peoples; now it became a matter of theory and belief. And from this resulted a great change of attitude towards the problems of colonial administration. The American problem in the eighteenth century had arisen ultimately out of the demand of the Americans for unqualified and responsible control over their own affairs: the attitude of the Englishman in reply to this demand (though he never clearly analysed it) was, in effect, that self-government was a good and desirable thing, but that on the scale on which the Americans claimed it, it would be fatal to the unity of the Empire, and the unity of the Empire must come first. Faced by similar problems in the nineteenth century, the Englishman's response generally was that self-government on the fullest scale was the right of all who were fit to exercise it, and the most satisfactory working solution of political problems. Therefore the right must be granted; and the unity of the Empire must take care of itself. No doubt this attitude was more readily adopted because of the widespread belief that in fact the colonies would all sooner or later cut their connection with the mother-country. But it was fully shared by men who did not hold this view, and who believed strongly in the possibility and desirability of maintaining imperial unity. It was shared, for example, by Wakefield, a convinced imperialist if ever there was one, and by that great colonial administrator, Sir George Grey. It was shared by Lord Durham and by Lord John Russell, who were largely responsible for the adoption of the new policy. Their belief and hope was that the common possession of free institutions of kindred types would in fact form the most effective tie between the lands which enjoyed them. This hope obtained an eloquent expression in the speech in which, in 1852, Russell introduced the bill for granting to the Australian colonies self-government on such a scale as amounted almost to independence. It is not true, as is sometimes said, that the self-governing institutions of the colonies were established during this period owing to the indifference of the home authorities, and their readiness to put an end to the connection. The new policy of these years was deliberately adopted; and although its acceptance by parliament was rendered easier by the prevalence of disbelief in the permanence of the imperial tie, yet, on the part of the responsible men, it was due to far-sighted statesmanship.

The critical test of the new colonial policy, and the most dramatic demonstration of its efficacy, were afforded by Canada, where, during the thirties, the conditions which preceded the revolt of the American colonies were being reproduced with curious exactness. The self-governing institutions established in the Canadian colonies in 1791 very closely resembled those of the American colonies before the revolution: they gave to the representative houses control over taxation and legislation, but neither control over, nor responsibility for, the executive. And the same results were following. Incomplete self-government was striving after its own fulfilment: the denial of responsibility was producing irresponsibility. These was the same unceasing friction between governors and their councils on the one hand, and the representative bodies on the other hand; and the assemblies were showing the same unreasonableness in refusing to meet manifest public obligations. This state of things was becoming steadily more acute in all the colonies, but it was at its worst in the province of Quebec, where the constitutional friction was embittered by a racial conflict, the executive body being British, while the great majority of the assembly was French; and the conflict was producing a very dangerous alienation between the two peoples. The French colonists had quite forgotten the gratitude they had once felt for the maintenance of their religion and of their social organisation, and there was a strong party among them who were bent upon open revolt, and hoped to be able to establish a little isolated French community upon the St. Lawrence. This party of hotheads got the upper hand, and their agitation culminated in the rebellion of Papineau in 1837. In the other colonies, and especially in Upper Canada, the conditions were almost equally ominous; when Papineau revolted in Quebec, William Mackenzie led a sympathetic rising in Ontario. The situation was quite as alarming as the situation in the American colonies had been in 1775. It is true that the risings were easily put down. But mere repression formed no solution, any more than a British victory in 1775 would have formed a solution of the American question.

Realising this, the Whig government sent out Lord Durham, one of their own number, to report on the whole situation. Durham was one of the most advanced Liberals in Britain, a convinced believer in the virtues of self-government, and he took out with him two of the ablest advocates of scientific colonisation, Edward Gibbon Wakefield and Charles Buller. Durham's administrative work was not a success: his high-handed deportation of some of the rebel leaders was strongly condemned, and he was very quickly recalled. But he had had time to study and understand the situation, and he presented a masterly Report on Canada, which is one of the classics in the history of British imperialism. His explanation of the unhappy condition of Canadian politics was not (as some were tempted to say) that the colonists had been given too much liberty, but that they had not been given enough. They must be made to feel their responsibility for the working of the laws which they adopted, and for the welfare of the whole community. As for the conflict of races, its only cure was that both should be made to feel their common responsibility for the destinies of the community in which both must remain partners.

Lord Durham's recommendations were fully carried into effect, partly in the Canada Act of 1840, but more especially by a simple instruction issued to governors, that their ministries must henceforward be chosen, in the British fashion, on the ground that they commanded the support of a majority in the elected house; and that the governors themselves must be guided by their advice. A crucial test of this new policy came in 1849, when the ministers and the parliamentary majority proposed to vote compensation for property destroyed in 1837. This to many seemed compensation for rebels, and the indignant loyalists were urgent that the governor, Lord Elgin, should veto it. He firmly declined to do so; and thus gave an invaluable lesson to both parties. The Canadian people, acting through their representatives, were now responsible for their actions. If they chose to vote for irresponsible and dangerous devices, they must henceforward realise that they must themselves answer for the consequences.

Thus, within a few years of the outbreak of rebellion in two provinces, full power had been entrusted to the rebels themselves. It was a daring policy, only to be justified by a very confident belief in the virtues of self-government. But it was completely and triumphantly successful. Henceforward friction between the Canadian colonies and the mother-country ceased: if there were grounds for complaint in the state of Canadian affairs, the Canadians must now blame their own ministers, and the remedy lay in their own hands. And what was the outcome? Twenty years later the various colonies, once as full of mutual jealousies as the American colonies had been before 1775, began to discuss the possibility of federation. With the cordial approval and co-operation of the home government, they drew up a scheme for the formation of a united Dominion of Canada, including distant British Columbia and the coastal colonies of Nova Scotia, New Brunswick, and Prince Edward Island; and the adoption of this scheme, in 1867, turned Canada from a bundle of separate settlements into a great state. To this state the home government later made over the control of all the vast and rich lands of the North-West, and so the destinies of half a continent passed under its direction. It was a charge, the magnitude and challenge of which could not but bring forth all that there was of statesmanship among the Canadian people; and it has not failed to do so.

One feature of Canadian constitutional development remains to be noted. It might have been expected that the Canadians would have been tempted to follow the political model of their great neighbour the United States; and if their development had been the outcome of friction with the mother-country, no doubt they would have done so. But they preferred to follow the British model. The keynote of the American system is division of power: division between the federal government and the state governments, which form mutual checks upon one another; division between the executive and the legislature, which are independent of one another at once in the states and in the federal government, both being directly elected by popular vote. The keynote of the British system is concentration of responsibility by the subordination of the executive to the legislature. The Canadians adopted the British principle: what had formerly been distinct colonies became, not 'states' but 'provinces,' definitely subordinated to the supreme central government; and whether in the federal or in the provincial system, the control of government by the representative body was finally established. This concord with the British system is a fact of real import. It means that the political usages of the home-country and the great Dominion are so closely assimilated that political co-operation between them is far easier than it otherwise might be; it increases the possibility of a future link more intimate than that of mere co-operation.

Not less whole-hearted or generous than the treatment of the problems of Canadian government was the treatment of the same problem in Australia. Here, as a matter of course, all the colonies had been endowed, at the earliest possible date, with the familiar system of representative but not responsible government. No such acute friction as had occurred in Canada had yet shown itself, though signs of its development were not lacking. But in 1852 an astonishing step was taken by the British parliament: the various Australian colonies were empowered to elect single-chamber constituent assemblies to decide the forms of government under which they wished to live. They decided in every case to reproduce as nearly as possible the British system: legislatures of two chambers, with ministries responsible to them. Thus, in Australia as in Canada, the daughter-peoples were made to feel the community of their institutions with those of the mother-country, and the possibility of intimate and easy co-operation was increased. Two years later, in 1854, New Zealand was endowed with the same system. Among all the British realms in which the white man was predominant, only South Africa was as yet excluded from this remarkable development. The reasons for this exclusion we have already noted: its consequences will occupy our attention in later pages.

Very manifestly the empire which was developing on such lines was not an empire in the old sense—a dominion imposed by force upon unwilling subjects. That old word, which has been used in so many senses, was being given a wholly new connotation. It was being made to mean a free partnership of self-governing peoples, held together not by force, but in part by common interests, and in a still higher degree by common sentiment and the possession of the same institutions of liberty.

In the fullest sense, however, this new conception of empire applied only to the group of the great self-governing colonies. There were many other regions, even before 1878, included within the British Empire, though as yet it had not incorporated those vast protectorates over regions peopled by backward races which have been added during the last generation. There were tropical settlements like British Honduras, British Guiana, Sierra Leone, and Cape Coast Castle; there were many West Indian Islands, and scattered possessions like Mauritius and Hong-Kong and Singapore and the Straits Settlements; there were garrison towns or coaling-stations like Gibraltar, Malta, Aden, St. Helena. To none of these were the institutions of full responsible self-government granted. Some of them possessed representative institutions without responsible ministries; in others the governor was assisted by a nominated council, intended to express local opinion, but not elected by the inhabitants; in yet others the governor ruled autocratically. But in all these cases the ultimate control of policy was retained by the home government. And in this general category, as yet, the South African colonies were included. Why were these distinctions drawn? Why did the generation of British statesmen, who had dealt so generously with the demand for self-government in Canada and Australia, stop short and refuse to carry out their principles in these other cases?

It is characteristic of British politics that they are never merely or fully logical, and that even when political doctrines seem to enjoy the most complete ascendancy, they are never put into effect without qualifications or exceptions. The exceptions already named to the establishment of full self-government were due to many and varying causes. In the first place, there was in most of these cases no effective demand for full self-government; and it may safely be asserted that any community in which there is no demand for self-governing institutions is probably not in a condition to work them with effect. Some of these possessions were purely military posts, like Gibraltar and Aden, and were necessarily administered as such. Others were too small and weak to dream of assuming the full privileges. But in the majority of cases one outstanding common feature will appear on closer analysis. Nearly all these territories were tropical or semi-tropical lands, whose British inhabitants were not permanent settlers, but were present solely for the purposes of trade or other exploitation, while the bulk of the population consisted of backward peoples, whose traditions and civilisation rendered their effective participation in public affairs quite impracticable. In such cases, to have given full political power to the small and generally shifting minority of white men would have been to give scope to many evils; and to have enfranchised, on a mere theory, the mass of the population would have been to produce still worse results. It would have sentenced these communities to the sort of fate which has befallen the beautiful island of Hayti, where the self-government of a population of emancipated negro slaves has brought nothing but anarchy and degradation. In such conditions the steady Reign of Law is the greatest boon that can be given to white settlers and coloured subjects alike; and the final authority is rightly retained by the home government, inspired, as British opinion has long required that it should be, by the principle that the rights of the backward peoples must be safeguarded. Under this system, both law and a real degree of liberty are made possible; whereas under a doctrinaire application of the theory of self-government, both would vanish.

But there remains the vast dominion of India, which falls neither into the one category nor into the other. Though there are many primitive and backward elements among its vast population, there are also peoples and castes whose members are intellectually capable of meeting on equal terms the members of any of the ruling races of the West. Yet during this age, when self-government on the amplest scale was being extended to the chief regions of the British Empire, India, the greatest dominion of them all, did not obtain the gift of representative institutions even on the most modest scale. Why was this?

It was not because the ruling race was hostile to the idea, or desired merely to retain its own ascendancy. On the contrary, both in Britain and among the best of the British administrators in India, it was increasingly held that the only ultimate justification for the British power in India would be that under its guidance the Indian peoples should be gradually enabled to govern themselves. As early as 1824, when in Europe sheer reaction was at its height, this view was being strongly urged by one of the greatest of Anglo-Indian administrators, Sir Thomas Munro, a soldier of distinction, then serving as governor of Madras. 'We should look upon India,' he wrote, 'not as a temporary possession, but as one which is to be maintained permanently, until the natives shall have abandoned most of their superstitions and prejudices, and become sufficiently enlightened to frame a regular government for themselves, and to conduct and preserve it. Whenever such a time shall arrive, it will probably be best for both countries that the British control over India should be gradually withdrawn. That the desirable change contemplated may in some after age be effected in India, there is no cause to despair. Such a change was at one time in Britain itself at least as hopeless as it is here. When we reflect how much the character of nations has always been influenced by that of governments, and that some, once the most cultivated, have sunk into barbarism, while others, formerly the rudest, have attained the highest point of civilisation, we shall see no reason to doubt that if we pursue steadily the proper measures, we shall in time so far improve the character of our Indian subjects as to make them able to govern and protect themselves.'

In other words, self-government was the desirable end to be pursued in India as elsewhere; but in India there were many and grave obstacles to its efficient working, which could only slowly be overcome. In the first place, India is more deeply divided in race, language, and religion than any other region of the world. Nowhere else is there such a medley of peoples of every grade of development, from the almost savage Bhil to the cultivated and high-bred Brahmin or Rajput or Mahomedan chief. There are sharp regional differences, as great as those between the European countries; but cutting across these there are everywhere the rigid and impermeable distinctions of caste, which have no parallel anywhere else in the world. The experience of the Austro-Hungarian Empire, whose confusion of races is simplicity itself in comparison with the chaos of India, affords a significant demonstration of the fact that parliamentary institutions, if they are established among deeply divided peoples, must almost inevitably be exploited for the purpose of racial ascendancy by the most vigorous or the best-organised elements among the people; and a very ugly tyranny is apt to result, as it has resulted in Austro-Hungary. This consequence would almost certainly follow the establishment of a full representative system in India. In the cities of mediaeval Italy, when the conflict of parties became so acute that neither side could expect justice from the other, the practice grew up of electing a podesta from some foreign city to act as an impartial arbiter. The British power in India has played the part of a podesta in restraining and mediating between the conflicting peoples and religions of India.

But again (and this is even more fundamental), for thousands of years the history of India has been one long story of conquests and tyrannies by successive ruling races. Always Might has been Right, so that the lover of righteousness could only pursue it, like the mediaeval ascetic, by cutting himself off from the world, abjuring all social ties, and immolating the flesh in order to live by the spirit. Always Law had been, in the last resort, the Will of the Stronger, not the decree of impartial justice. Always the master-races, the predatory bands, the ruling castes, had expected to receive, and the mass of the people had been accustomed to give, the most abject submission; and these habits were difficult to overcome. 'In England,' says Sir Thomas Munro, 'the people resist oppression, and it is their spirit which gives efficacy to the law: in India the people rarely resist oppression, and the law intended to secure them from it can therefore derive no aid from themselves. ... It is in vain to caution them against paying by telling them that the law is on their side, and will support them in refusing to comply with unauthorised demands. All exhortations on this head are thrown away, and after listening to them they will the very next day submit to extortion as quietly as before.' How could representative institutions be expected to work under such conditions? They would have lacked the very foundation upon which alone they can firmly rest: respect for law, and public co-operation in the enforcement of it. Thus the supreme service which the government of India could render to its people was the establishment and maintenance of the Reign of Law, and of the liberty which it shelters. In such conditions representative government would be liable to bring, not liberty, but anarchy and the renewal of lawless oppression.

But although the extension of the representative system to India neither was nor could be attempted in this age, very remarkable advances were made towards turning India in a real sense into a self-governing country. It ceased to be regarded or treated as a subject dominion existing solely for the advantage of its conquerors. That had always been its fate in all the long centuries of its history; and in the first period of British rule the trading company which had acquired this amazing empire had naturally regarded it as primarily a source of profit. In 1833 the company was forbidden to engage in trade, and the profit-making motive disappeared. The shareholders still continued to receive a fixed dividend out of the Indian revenues, but this may be compared to a fixed debt-charge, an annual payment for capital expended in the past; and it came to an end when the company was abolished in 1858. Apart from this dividend, no sort of tribute was exacted from India by the ruling power. India was not even required to contribute to the upkeep of the navy, which protected her equally with the rest of the Empire, or of the diplomatic service, which was often concerned with her interests. She paid for the small army which guarded her frontiers; but if any part of it was borrowed for service abroad, its whole pay and charges were met by Britain. She paid the salaries and pensions of the handful of British administrators who conducted her government, but this was a very small charge in comparison with the lavish outlay of the native princes whom they had replaced. India had become a self-contained state, whose whole resources were expended exclusively upon her own needs, and expended with the most scrupulous honesty, and under the most elaborate safeguards.

They were expended, moreover, especially during the later part of this period, largely in equipping her with the material apparatus of modern civilisation. Efficient police, great roads, a postal service cheaper than that of any other country, a well-planned railway system, and, above all, a gigantic system of irrigation which brought under cultivation vast regions hitherto desert—these were some of the boons acquired by India during the period. They were rendered possible partly by the economical management of her finances, partly by the liberal expenditure of British capital. Above all, the period saw the beginning of a system of popular education, of which the English language became the main vehicle, because none of the thirty-eight recognised vernacular tongues of India either possessed the necessary literature, or could be used as a medium for instruction in modern science. In 1858 three universities were established; and although their system was ill-devised, under the malign influence of the analogy of London University, a very large and increasing number of young graduates, trained for modern occupations, began to filter into Indian society, and to modify its point of view. All speaking and writing English, and all trained in much the same body of ideas, they possessed a similarity of outlook and a vehicle of communication such as had never before linked together the various races and castes of India.

This large and growing class, educated in some measure in the learning of the West, formed already, at the end of the period, a very important new element in the life of India. They were capable of criticising the work of their government; they were not without standards of comparison by which to measure its achievements; and, aided by the large freedom granted to the press under the British system, they were able to begin the creation of an intelligent public opinion, which was apt, in its first movements, to be ill-guided and rash, but which was nevertheless a healthy development. That this newly created class of educated men should produce a continual stream of criticism, and that it should even stimulate into existence public discontents, is by no means a condemnation of the system of government which has made these developments possible. On the contrary, it is a proof that the system has had an invigorating effect. For the existence and the expression of discontent is a sign of life; it means that there is an end of that utter docility which marks a people enslaved body and soul. India has never been more prosperous than she is to-day; she has never before known so impartial a system of justice as she now possesses; and these are legitimate grounds of pride to her rulers. But they may even more justly pride themselves upon the fact that in all her history India has never been so frankly and incessantly critical of her government as she is to-day; never so bold in the aspirations for the future which her sons entertain.

The creation of the new class of Western-educated Indians also facilitated another development which the British government definitely aimed at encouraging: the participation of Indians in the conduct of administration in their own land. The Act of 1833 had laid it down as a fundamental principle that 'no native of the said territories ... shall by reason only of his religion, place of birth, descent, or any of them, be disabled from holding any place, office, or employment.' The great majority of the minor administrative posts had always been held by Indians; but until 1833 it had been held that the maintenance of British supremacy required that the higher offices should be reserved to members of the ruling race. This restriction was now abolished; but it was not until the development of the educational system had produced a body of sufficiently trained men that the new principle could produce appreciable results; and even then, the deficiencies of an undeveloped system of training, combined with the racial and religious jealousies which the government of India must always keep in mind, imposed limitations upon the rapid increase of the number of Indians holding the higher posts. Still, the principle had been laid down, and was being acted upon. And that also constituted a great step towards self-government.

India in 1878 was governed, under the terms of a code of law based upon Indian custom, by a small body of British officials, among whom leading Indians were gradually taking their place, and who worked in detail through an army of minor officials, nearly all of Indian birth, and selected without regard to race or creed. She was a self-contained country whose whole resources were devoted to her own needs. She was prospering to a degree unexampled in her history; she had achieved a political unity never before known to her; she had been given the supreme boon of a just and impartial law, administered without fear or favour; and she had enjoyed a long period of peace, unbroken by any attack from external foes. Here also, as fully as in the self-governing colonies, membership of the British Empire did not mean subjection to the selfish dominion of a master, or the subordination to that master's interests of the vital interests of the community. It meant the establishment among a vast population of the essential gifts of Western civilisation, rational law, and the liberty which exists under its shelter. Empire had come to mean, not merely domination pursued for its own sake, but trusteeship for the extension of civilisation.

The period of practical British monopoly, 1815-1878, had thus brought about a very remarkable transformation in the character of the British Empire. It had greatly increased in extent, and by every test of area, population, and natural resources, it was beyond comparison the greatest power that had ever existed in the world. But its organisation was of an extreme laxity; it possessed no real common government; and its principal members were united rather by a community of institutions and ideas than by any formal ties. Moreover, it presented a more amazing diversity of racial types, of religions, and of grades of civilisation, than any other political fabric which had existed in history. Its development had assuredly brought about a very great expansion of the ideas of Western civilisation over the face of the globe, and, above all, a remarkable diffusion of the institutions of political liberty. But it remained to be proved whether this loosely compacted bundle of states possessed any real unity, or would be capable of standing any severe strain. The majority of observers, both in Britain itself and throughout the world, would have been inclined, in 1878, to give a negative answer to these questions.

VII
THE ERA OF THE WORLD-STATES, 1878-1900

The Congress of Berlin in 1878 marks the close of the era of nationalist revolutions and wars in Europe. By the same date all the European states had attained to a certain stability in their constitutional systems. With equal definiteness this year may be said to mark the opening of a new era in the history of European imperialism; an era of eager competition for the control of the still unoccupied regions of the world, in which the concerns of remote lands suddenly became matters of supreme moment to the great European powers, and the peace of the world was endangered by questions arising in China or Siam, in Morocco or the Soudan, or the islands of the Pacific. The control of Europe over the non-European world was in a single generation completed and confirmed. And the most important of the many questions raised by this development was the question whether the spirit in which this world-supremacy of Europe was to be wielded should be the spirit which long experience had inspired in the oldest of the colonising nations, the spirit of trusteeship on behalf of civilisation; or whether it was to be the old, brutal, and sterile spirit of mere domination for its own sake.

On a superficial view the most obvious feature of this strenuous period was that all the remaining unexploited regions of the world were either annexed by one or other of the great Western states, or were driven to adopt, with greater or less success, the modes of organisation of the West. But what was far more important than any new demarcation of the map was that not only the newly annexed lands, but also the half-developed territories of earlier European dominions, were with an extraordinary devouring energy penetrated during this generation by European traders and administrators, equipped with railways, steam-boats, and all the material apparatus of modern life, and in general organised and exploited for the purposes of industry and trade. This astonishing achievement was almost as thorough as it was swift. And its result was, not merely that the political control of Europe over the backward regions of the world was strengthened and secured by these means, but that the whole world was turned into a single economic and political unit, no part of which could henceforth dwell in isolation. This might have meant that we should have been brought nearer to some sort of world-order; but unhappily the spirit in which the great work was undertaken by some, at least, of the nations which participated in it has turned this wonderful achievement into a source of bitterness and enmity, and led the world in the end to the tragedy and agony of the Great War.

The causes of this gigantic outpouring of energy were manifold. The main impelling forces were perhaps economic rather than political. But the economic needs of this strenuous age might have been satisfied without resort to the brutal arbitrament of war: their satisfaction might even have been made the means of diminishing the danger of war. It was the interpretation of these economic needs in terms of an unhappy political theory which has led to the final catastrophe.

On a broad view, the final conquest of the world by European civilisation was made possible, and indeed inevitable, by the amazing development of the material aspects of that civilisation during the nineteenth century; by the progressive command over the forces of nature which the advance of science had placed in the hands of man, by the application of science to industry in the development of manufacturing methods and of new modes of communication, and by the intricate and flexible organisation of modern finance. These changes were already in progress before 1878, and were already transforming the face of the world. Since 1878 they have gone forward with such accelerating speed that we have been unable to appreciate the significance of the revolution they were effecting. We have been carried off our feet; and have found it impossible to adjust our moral and political ideas to the new conditions.

The great material achievements of the last two generations have been mainly due to an intense concentration and specialisation of functions among both men of thought and men of action. But the result of this has been that there have been few to attempt the vitally important task of appreciating the movement of our civilisation as a whole, and of endeavouring to determine how far the political conceptions inherited from an earlier age were valid in the new conditions. For under the pressure of the great transformation political forces also have been transformed, and in all countries political thought is baffled and bewildered by the complexity of the problems by which it is faced. To this in part we owe the dimness of vision which overtook us as we went whirling together towards the great catastrophe. It is only in the glare of a world-conflagration that we begin to perceive, in something like their true proportions, the great forces and events which have been shaping our destinies. In the future, if the huge soulless mechanism which man has created is not to get out of hand and destroy him, we must abandon that contempt for the philosopher and the political thinker which we have latterly been too ready to express, and we must recognise that the task of analysing and relating to one another the achievements of the past and the problems of the present is at least as important as the increase of our knowledge and of our dangerous powers by intense and narrow concentration within very limited fields of thought and work.

In the meantime we must observe (however briefly and inadequately), how the dazzling advances of science and industry have affected the conquest of the world by European civilisation, and why it has come about that instead of leading to amity and happiness, they have brought us to the most hideous catastrophe in human history.

Science and industry, in the first place, made the conquest and organisation of the world easy. In the first stages of the expansion of Europe the material superiority of the West had unquestionably afforded the means whereby its political ideas and institutions could be made operative in new fields. The invention of ocean-going ships, the use of the mariner's compass, the discovery of the rotundity of the earth, the development of firearms — these were the things which made possible the creation of the first European empires; though these purely material advantages could have led to no stable results unless they had been wielded by peoples possessing a real political capacity. In the same way the brilliant triumphs of modern engineering have alone rendered possible the rapid conquest and organisation of huge undeveloped areas; the deadly precision of Western weapons has made the Western peoples irresistible; the wonderful progress of medical science has largely overcome the barriers of disease which long excluded the white man from great regions of the earth; and the methods of modern finance, organising and making available the combined credit of whole communities, have provided the means for vast enterprises which without them could never have been undertaken.

Then, in the next place, science has found uses for many commodities which were previously of little value, and many of which are mainly produced in the undeveloped regions of the earth. Some of these, like rubber, or nitrates, or mineral and vegetable oils, have rapidly become quite indispensable materials, consumed by the industrial countries on an immense scale. Accordingly, the more highly industrialised a country is, the more dependent it must be upon supplies drawn from all parts of the world; not only supplies of food for the maintenance of its teeming population, but, even more, supplies of material for its industries. The days when Europe, or even America, was self-sufficient are gone for ever. And in order that these essential supplies may be available, it has become necessary that all the regions which produce them should be brought under efficient administration. The anarchy of primitive barbarism cannot be allowed to stand in the way of access to these vital necessities of the new world-economy. It is merely futile for well-meaning sentimentalists to talk of the wickedness of invading the inalienable rights of the primitive occupants of these lands: for good or for ill, the world has become a single economic unit, and its progress cannot be stopped out of consideration for the time-honoured usages of uncivilised and backward tribes. Of course it is our duty to ensure that these simple folks are justly treated, led gently into civilisation, and protected from the iniquities of a mere ruthless exploitation, such as, in some regions, we have been compelled to witness. But Western civilisation has seized the reins of the world, and it will not be denied. Its economic needs drive it to undertake the organisation of the whole world. What we have to secure is that its political principles shall be such as will ensure that its control will be a benefit to its subjects as well as to itself. But the development of scientific industry has made European control and civilised administration inevitable throughout the world.

It did not, however, necessarily follow from these premises that the great European states which did not already possess extra-European territories were bound to acquire such lands. So far as their purely economic needs were concerned, it would have been enough that they should have freedom of access, on equal terms with their neighbours, to the sources of the supplies they required. It is quite possible, as events have shown, for a European state to attain very great success in the industrial sphere without possessing any political control over the lands from which its raw materials are drawn, or to which its finished products are sold. Norway has created an immense shipping industry without owning a single port outside her own borders. The manufactures of Switzerland are as thriving as these of any European country, though Switzerland does not possess any colonies. Germany herself, the loudest advocate of the necessity of political control as the basis of economic prosperity, has found it possible to create a vast and very prosperous industry, though her colonial possessions have been small, and have contributed scarcely at all to her wealth. Her merchants and capitalists have indeed found the most profitable fields for their enterprises, not in their own colonies, which they have on the whole tended to neglect, but in a far greater degree in South and Central America, and in India and the other vast territories of the British Empire, which have been open to them as freely as to British merchants. All that the prosperity of European industry required was that the sources of supply should be under efficient administration, and that access to them should be open. And these conditions were fulfilled, before the great rush began, over the greater part of the earth. If in 1878, when the European nations suddenly awoke to the importance of the non-European world, they had been able to agree upon some simple principle which would have secured equal treatment to all, how different would have been the fate of Europe and the world! If it could have been laid down, as a principle of international law, that in every area whose administration was undertaken by a European state, the 'open door' should be secured for the trade of all nations equally, and that this rule should continue in force until the area concerned acquired the status of a distinctly organised state controlling its own fiscal system, the industrial communities would have felt secure, the little states quite as fully as the big states. Moreover, since, under these conditions, the annexation of territory by a European state would not have threatened the creation of a monopoly, but would have meant the assumption of a duty on behalf of civilisation, the acrimonies and jealousies which have attended the process of partition would have been largely conjured away. In 1878 such a solution would have presented few difficulties. For at that date the only European state which controlled large undeveloped areas was Britain; and Britain, as we have seen, had on her own account arrived at this solution, and had administered, as she still administers, all those regions of her Empire which do not possess self-governing rights in the spirit of the principle we have suggested.

Why was it that this solution, or some solution on these lines, was not then adopted, and had no chance of being adopted? It was because the European states, and first and foremost among them Germany, were still dominated by a political theory which forbade their taking such a view. We may call this theory the Doctrine of Power. It is the doctrine that the highest duty of every state is to aim at the extension of its own power, and that before this duty every other consideration must give way. The Doctrine of Power has never received a more unflinching expression than it received from the German Treitschke, whose influence was at its height during the years of the great rush for extra-European possessions. The advocate of the Doctrine of Power is not, and cannot be, satisfied with equality of opportunity; he demands supremacy, he demands monopoly, he demands the means to injure and destroy his rivals. It would not be just to say that this doctrine was influential only in Germany; it was in some degree potent everywhere, especially in this period, which was the period par excellence of 'imperialism' in the bad sense of the term. But it is certainly true that no state has ever been so completely dominated by it as Germany; and no state less than Britain. It was in the light of this doctrine that the demands of the new scientific industry were interpreted. Hag-ridden by this conception, when the statesmen of Europe awoke to the importance of the non-European world, it was not primarily the economic needs of their countries that they thought of, for these were, on the whole, not inadequately met: what struck their imagination was that, in paying no attention to the outer world, they had missed great opportunities of increasing their power. This oversight, they resolved, must be rectified before it was too late.

For when the peoples of Western and Central Europe, no longer engrossed by the problems of Nationalism and Liberalism, cast their eyes over the world, lo! the scale of things seemed to have changed. Just as, in the fifteenth century, civilisation had suddenly passed from the stage of the city-state or the feudal principality to the stage of the great nation-state, so now, while the European peoples were still struggling to realise their nationhood, civilisation seemed to have stolen a march upon them, and to have advanced once more, this time into the stage of the world-state. For to the east of the European nations lay the vast Russian Empire, stretching from Central Europe across Asia to the Pacific; and in the west the American Republic extended from ocean to ocean, across three thousand miles of territory; and between these and around them spread the British Empire, sprawling over the whole face of the globe, on every sea and in every continent. In contrast with these giant empires, the nation-states of Europe felt themselves out of scale, just as the Italian cities in the sixteenth century must have felt themselves out of scale in comparison with the new nation-states of Spain and France. To achieve the standard of the world-state, to make their own nations the controlling factors in wide dominions which should include territories and populations of varied types, became the ambition of the most powerful European states. A new political ideal had captivated the mind of Europe.

These powerful motives were reinforced by others which arose from the development of affairs within Europe itself. In the first place, the leading European states had by 1878 definitely abandoned that tendency towards free trade which had seemed to be increasing in strength during the previous generation; and, largely in the hope of combating the overwhelming mercantile and industrial supremacy of Britain, had adopted the fiscal policy of protection. The ideal of the protectionist creed is national self-sufficiency in the economic sphere. But, as we have seen, economic self-sufficiency was no longer attainable in the conditions of modern industry by any European state. Only by large foreign annexations, especially in the tropical regions, did it seem possible of achievement. But when a protectionist state begins to acquire territory, the anticipation that it will use its power to exclude or destroy the trade of its rivals must drive other states to safeguard themselves by still further annexations. It was, indeed, this fear which mainly drove Britain, in spite of, or perhaps because of, her free trade theories, into a series of large annexations in regions where her trade had been hitherto predominant.

Again, the most perturbing feature of the relations between the European powers also contributed to produce an eagerness for colonial possessions. Europe had entered upon the era of huge national armies; the example of Prussia, and the rancours which had been created by her policy, had set all the nations arming themselves. They had learned to measure their strength by their available man-power, and in two ways the desire to increase the reserve of military manhood formed a motive for colonisation. In the first place, the surplus manhood of a nation was lost to it if it was allowed to pass under an alien flag by emigration. Those continental states from which emigration took place on a large scale began to aspire after the possession of colonies of their own, where their emigrants could still be kept under control, and remain subject to the obligations of service. Germany, the state which beyond all others measures its strength by its fighting man-power, was most affected by this motive, which formed the chief theme of the colonial school among her politicians and journalists, and continued to be so even when the stream of her emigrants had dwindled to very small proportions. In a less degree, Italy was influenced by the same motive. In the second place, conquered subjects even of backward races might be made useful for the purposes of war. This motive appealed most strongly to France. Her home population was stationary. She lived in constant dread of a new onslaught from her formidable neighbour; and she watched with alarm the rapid increase of that neighbour's population, and the incessant increases in the numbers of his armies. At a later date Germany also began to be attracted by the possibility of drilling and arming, among the negroes of Central Africa, or the Turks of Asia Minor, forces which might aid her to dominate the world.

Thus the political situation in Europe had a very direct influence upon the colonising activity of this period. The dominant fact of European politics during this generation was the supreme prestige and influence of Germany, who, not content with an unquestioned military superiority to any other power, had buttressed herself by the formation (1879 and 1882) of the most formidable standing alliance that has ever existed in European history, and completely dominated European politics. France, having been hurled from the leadership of Europe in 1870, dreaded nothing so much as the outbreak of a new European war, in which she must be inevitably involved, and in which she might be utterly ruined. She strove to find a compensation for her wounded pride in colonial adventures, and therefore became, during the first part of the period, the most active of the powers in this field. She was encouraged to adopt this policy by Bismarck, partly in the hope that she might thus forget Alsace, partly in order that she might be kept on bad terms with Britain, whose interests seemed to be continually threatened by her colonising activity. But she hesitated to take a very definite line in regard to territories that lay close to Europe and might involve European complications.

Bismarck himself took little interest in colonial questions, except in so far as they could be used as a means of alienating the other powers from one another, and so securing the European supremacy of Germany. He therefore at first made no attempt to use the dominant position of Germany as a means of acquiring extra-European dominions. But the younger generation in Germany was far from sharing this view. It was determined to win for Germany a world-empire, and in 1884 and the following years — rather late in the day, when most of the more desirable territories were already occupied — it forced Bismarck to annex large areas. After Bismarck's fall, in 1890, this party got the upper hand in German politics, and the creation of a great world-empire became, as we shall see, the supreme aim of William II. and his advisers. The formidable and threatening power of Germany began to be systematically employed not merely for the maintenance of supremacy in Europe, which could be secured by peaceful means, but for the acquisition of a commanding position in the outer world; and since this could only be attained by violence, the world being now almost completely partitioned, the new policy made Germany the source of unrest and apprehension, as she had earlier been, and still continued to be, the main cause of the burden of military preparation in Europe.

Among the other powers which participated in the great partition, Russia continued her pressure in two of the three directions which she had earlier followed-south-eastwards in Central Asia, eastwards towards China. In both directions her activity aroused the nervous fears of Britain, while her pressure upon China helped to bring Japan into the ranks of the militant and aggressive powers. But Russia took no interest in the more distant quarters of the world. Nor did Austria, though during these years her old ambition to expand south-eastwards at the expense of Turkey and the Balkan peoples revived under German encouragement. Italy, having but recently achieved national unity and taken her place among the Great Powers, felt that she could not be left out of the running, now that extra-European possessions had come to appear an almost essential mark of greatness among states; and, disappointed of Tunis, she endeavoured to find compensation on the shores of the Red Sea. Spain and Portugal, in the midst of all these eager rivalries, were tempted to furbish up their old and half-dormant claims. Even the United States of America joined in the rush during the fevered period of the 'nineties.

Lastly, Britain, the oldest and the most fully endowed of all the colonising powers, was drawn, half unwilling, into the competition; and having an immense start over her rivals, actually acquired more new territory than any of them. She was, indeed, like the other states, passing through an 'imperialist' phase in these years. The value attached by other countries to oversea possessions awakened among the British people a new pride in their far-spread dominions. Disraeli, who was in the ascendant when the period opened, had forgotten his old opinion of the uselessness of colonies, and had become a prophet of Empire. An Imperial Federation Society was founded in 1878. The old unwillingness to assume new responsibilities died out, or diminished; and the rapid annexations of other states, especially France, in regions where British influence had hitherto been supreme, and whose chieftains had often begged in vain for British protection, aroused some irritation. The ebullient energy of the colonists themselves, especially in South Africa and Australia, demanded a forward policy. Above all, the fact that the European powers, now so eager for colonial possessions, had all adopted the protectionist policy aroused a fear lest British traders should find themselves shut out from lands whose trade had hitherto been almost wholly in their hands; and the militant and aggressive temper sometimes shown by the agents of these powers awakened some nervousness regarding the safety of the existing British possessions. Hence Britain, after a period of hesitancy, became as active as any of the other states in annexation. Throughout this period her main rival was France, whose new claims seemed to come in conflict with her own in almost every quarter of the globe. This rivalry produced acute friction, which grew in intensity until it reached its culminating point in the crisis of Fashoda in 1898, and was not removed until the settlement of 1904 solved all the outstanding difficulties. It would be quite untrue to say that Britain deliberately endeavoured to prevent or to check the rapid colonial expansion of France. The truth is that British trading interests had been predominant in many of the regions where the French were most active, and that the protectionist policy which France had adopted stimulated into a new life the ancient rivalry of these neighbour and sister nations. Towards the colonial ambitions of Germany, and still more of Italy, Britain was far more complaisant.

It is difficult to give in a brief space a clear summary of the extremely complicated events and intrigues of this vitally important period. But perhaps it will be easiest if we consider in turn the regions in which the strenuous rivalries of the powers displayed themselves. The most important was Africa, which lay invitingly near to Europe, and was the only large region of the world which was still for the most part unoccupied. Here all the competitors, save Russia, Japan, and America, played a part. Western Asia formed a second field, in which three powers only, Russia, Germany, and Britain, were immediately concerned. The Far East, where the vast Empire of China seemed to be falling into decrepitude, afforded the most vexed problems of the period. Finally, the Pacific Islands were the scene of an active though less intense rivalry.

It is a curious fact that Africa, the continent whose outline was the first outside of Europe itself to be fully mapped out by the European peoples, was actually the last to be effectively brought under the influence of European civilisation. This was because the coasts of Africa are for the most part inhospitable; its vast interior plateau is almost everywhere shut off either by belts of desert land, or by swampy and malarious regions along the coast; even its great rivers do not readily tempt the explorer inland, because their course is often interrupted by falls or rapids not far from their mouths, where they descend from the interior plateau to the coastal plain; and its inhabitants, warlike and difficult to deal with, are also peoples of few and simple wants, who have little to offer to the trader. Hence eight generations of European mariners had circumnavigated the continent without seriously attempting to penetrate its central mass; and apart from the Anglo-Dutch settlements at the Southern extremity, the French empire in Algeria in the north, a few trading centres on the West Coast, and some half-derelict Portuguese stations in Angola and Mozambique, the whole continent remained available for European exploitation in 1878.

What trade was carried on, except in Egypt, in Algeria, and in the immediate vicinity of the old French settlements on the West Coast, was mainly in the hands of British merchants. Over the greater part of the coastal belts only the British power was known to the native tribes and chieftains. Many of them (like the Sultan of Zanzibar and the chiefs of the Cameroons) had repeatedly begged to be taken under British protection, and had been refused. During the two generations before 1878 the interior of the continent had begun to be known. But except in the north and north-west, where French explorers and a few Germans had been active, the work had been mainly done by British travellers. Most of the great names of African exploration—Livingstone, Burton, Speke, Baker, Cameron and the Anglo-American Stanley—were British names. These facts, of course, gave to Britain, already so richly endowed, no sort of claim to a monopoly of the continent. But they naturally gave her a right to a voice in its disposal. Only the French had shown anything like the same activity, or had established anything like the same interests; and they were far behind their secular rivals.

But these facts bring out one feature which differentiated the settlement of Africa from that of any other region of the non-European world. It was not a gradual, but an extraordinarily rapid achievement. It was based not upon claims established by work already done, but, for the most part, upon the implicit assumption that extra-European empire was the due of the European peoples, simply because they were civilised and powerful. This was the justification, in a large degree, of all the European empires in Africa. But it was especially so in the case of the empire which Germany created in the space of three years. This empire was not the product of German enterprise in the regions included within it; it was the product of Germany's dominating position in Europe, and the expression of her resolve to create an external empire worthy of that position.

Africa falls naturally into two great regions. The northern coast, separated from the main mass of the continent by the broad belt of deserts which runs from the Atlantic to the Red Sea, has always been far more ultimately connected with the other Mediterranean lands than with the rest of Africa. Throughout the course of history, indeed, the northern coast-lands have belonged rather to the realms of Western or of Asiatic civilisation than to the primitive barbarism of the sons of Ham. In the days of the Carthaginians and of the Roman Empire, all these lands, from Egypt to Morocco, had known a high civilisation. They were racially as well as historically distinct from the rest of the continent. They had been in name part of the Turkish Empire, and any European interference in their affairs was as much a question of European politics as the problems of the Balkans. Two countries in this area fell under European direction during the period with which we are concerned, and in each case the effects upon European politics were very great. In 1881 France, with the deliberate encouragement of Bismarck, sent armies into Tunis, and assumed the protectorate of that misgoverned region. She had good grounds for her action. Not only had she large trade-interests in Tunis, but the country was separated from her earlier dominion in Algeria only by an artificial line, and its disorders increased the difficulty of developing the efficient administration which she had established there. Unhappily Italy also had interests in Tunis. There were more Italian than French residents in the country, which is separated from Sicily only by a narrow belt of sea. And Italy, who was beginning to conceive colonial ambitions, had not unnaturally marked down Tunis as her most obvious sphere of influence. The result was to create a long-lived ill-feeling between the two Latin countries. As a consequence of the annexation of Tunis, Italy was persuaded in the next year (1882) to join the Triple Alliance; and France, having burnt her fingers, became chary of colonial adventures in regions that were directly under the eye of Europe. Isolated, insecure, and eternally suspicious of Germany, she could not afford to be drawn into European quarrels. This is in a large degree the explanation of her vacillating action in regard to Egypt.

In Egypt the political influence of France had been preponderant ever since the time of Mehemet Ali; perhaps we should say, ever since the time of Napoleon. And political influence had been accompanied by trading and financial interests. France had a larger share of the trade of Egypt, and had lent more money to the ruling princes of the country, than any other country save England. She had designed and executed the Suez Canal. But this waterway, once opened, was used mainly by British ships on the way to India, Australia, and the Far East. It became a point of vital strategic importance to Britain, who, though she had opposed its construction, eagerly seized the chance of buying a great block of shares in the enterprise from the bankrupt Khedive. Thus

French and British interests in Egypt were equally great; greater than those of all the rest of Europe put together. When the native government of Egypt fell into bankruptcy (1876), the two powers set up a sort of condominium, or joint control of the finances, in order to ensure the payment of interest on the Egyptian debt held by their citizens. To bankruptcy succeeded political chaos; and it became apparent that if the rich land of Egypt was not to fall into utter anarchy, there must be direct European intervention. The two powers proposed to take joint action; the rest of Europe assented. But the Sultan of Turkey, as suzerain of Egypt, threatened to make difficulties. At the last moment France, fearful of the complications that might result, and resolute to avoid the danger of European war, withdrew from the project of joint intervention. Britain went on alone; and although she hoped and believed that she would quickly be able to restore order, and thereupon to evacuate the country, found herself drawn into a labour of reconstruction that could not be dropped. We shall in the next chapter have more to say on the British occupation of Egypt, as part of the British achievement during this period. In the meanwhile, its immediate result was continuous friction between France and Britain. France could not forgive herself or Britain for the opportunity which she had lost. The embitterment caused by the Egyptian question lasted throughout the period, and was not healed till the Entente of 1904. It intensified and exacerbated the rivalry of the two countries in other fields. It made each country incapable of judging fairly the actions of the other. To wounded and embittered France, the perfectly honest British explanations of the reasons for delay in evacuating Egypt seemed only so many evidences of hypocrisy masking greed. To Britain the French attitude seemed fractious and unreasonable, and she suspected in every French forward movement in other fields — notably in the Eastern Soudan and the upper valley of the Nile — an attempt to attack or undermine her. Thus Egypt, like Tunis, illustrated the influence of European politics in the extra-European field. The power that profited most was Germany, who had strengthened herself by drawing Italy into the Triple Alliance, and had kept France at her mercy by using colonial questions as a means of alienating her from her natural friends. It was, in truth, only from this point of view that colonial questions had any interest for Bismarck. He was, as he repeatedly asserted almost to the day of his death, 'no colony man.' But the time was at hand when he was to be forced out of this attitude. For already the riches of tropical Africa were beginning to attract the attention of Europe.

The most active and energetic of the powers in tropical Africa was France. From her ancient foothold at Senegal she was already, in the late 'seventies, pushing inland towards the upper waters of the Niger; while further south her vigorous explorer de Brazza was penetrating the hinterland behind the French coastal settlements north of the Congo mouth. Meanwhile the explorations of Livingstone and Stanley had given the world some conception of the wealth of the vast exterior. In 1876 Leopold, King of the Belgians, summoned a conference at Brussels to consider the possibility of setting the exploration and settlement of Africa upon an international basis. Its result was the formation of an International African Association, with branches in all the principal countries. But from the first the branches dropped all serious pretence of international action. They became (so far as they exercised any influence) purely national organisations for the purpose of acquiring the maximum amount of territory for their own states. And the central body, after attempting a few unsuccessful exploring expeditions, practically resolved itself into the organ of King Leopold himself, and aimed at creating a neutral state in Central Africa under his protection. In 1878 H. M. Stanley returned from the exploration of the Congo. He was at once invited by King Leopold to undertake the organisation of the Congo basin for his Association, and set out again for that purpose in 1879. But he soon found himself in conflict with the active French agents under de Brazza, who had made their way into the Congo valley from the north-west. And at the same time Portugal, reviving ancient and dormant claims, asserted that the Congo belonged to her. It was primarily to find a solution for these disputes that the Berlin Conference was summoned in December 1884. Meanwhile the rush for territory was going on furiously in other regions of Africa. Not only on the Congo, but on the Guinea Coast and its hinterland, France was showing an immense activity, and was threatening to reduce to small coastal enclaves the old British settlements on this coast. Only the energy shown by a group of British merchants, who formed themselves into a National African Company in 1881, and the vigorous action of their leader, Mr. (afterwards Sir) George Taubman Goldie, prevented the extrusion of British interests from the greater part of the Niger valley, where they had hitherto been supreme. In Madagascar, too, the ancient ambitions of France had revived. Though British trading and missionary activities in the island were at this date probably greater than French, France claimed large rights, especially in the north-east of the island. These claims drew her into a war with the native power of the Hovas, which began in 1883, and ended in 1885 with a vague recognition of French suzerainty. Again, Italy had, in 1883, obtained her first foothold in Eritrea, on the shore of the Red Sea. And Germany, also, had suddenly made up her mind to embark upon the career of empire. In 1883 the Bremen merchant, Luderitz, appeared in South-west Africa, where there were a few German mission stations and trading-centres, and annexed a large area which Bismarck was persuaded to take under the formal protection of Germany. This region had hitherto been vaguely regarded as within the British sphere, but though native princes, missionaries, and in 1868 even the Prussian government, had requested Britain to establish a formal protectorate, she had always declined to do so. In the next year another German agent, Dr. Nachtigal, was commissioned by the German government to report on German trade interests on the West Coast, and the British government was formally acquainted with his mission and requested to instruct its agents to assist him. The real purpose of the mission was shown when Nachtigal made a treaty with the King of Togoland, on the Guinea Coast, whereby he accepted German suzerainty. A week later a similar treaty was made with some of the native chiefs in the Cameroons. In this region British interests had hitherto been predominant, and the chiefs had repeatedly asked for British protection, which had always been refused. A little later the notorious Karl Peters, with a few companions disguised as working engineers, arrived at Zanzibar on the East Coast, with a commission from the German Colonial Society to peg out German claims. In the island of Zanzibar British interests had long been overwhelmingly predominant; and the Sultan, who had large and vague claims to supremacy over a vast extent of the mainland, had repeatedly asked the British government to take these regions under its protectorate. He had always been refused. Peters' luggage consisted largely of draft treaty-forms; and he succeeded in making treaties with native princes (usually unaware of the meaning of the documents they were signing) whereby some 60,000 square miles were brought under German control. The protectorate over these lands had not been accepted by the German government when the Conference of Berlin met. It was formally accepted in the next year (1885). Far from being opposed by Britain, the establishment of German power in East Africa was actually welcomed by the British government, whose foreign secretary, Earl Granville, wrote that his government 'views with favour these schemes, the realisation of which will entail the civilisation of large tracts over which hitherto no European influence has been exercised.' And when a group of British traders began to take action further north, in the territory which later became British East Africa, and in which Peters had done nothing, the British government actually consulted the German government before licensing their action. Thus before the meeting of the Conference of Berlin the foundations of the German empire in Africa were already laid; the outlines of the vast French empire in the north had begun to appear; and the curious dominion of Leopold of Belgium in the Congo valley had begun to take shape.

The Conference of Berlin (Dec. 1884-Feb. 1885), which marks the close of the first stage in the partition of Africa, might have achieved great things if it had endeavoured to lay down the principles upon which European control over backward peoples should be exercised. But it made no such ambitious attempt. It prescribed the rules of the game of empire-building, ordaining that all protectorates should be formally notified by the power which assumed them to the other powers, and that no annexation should be made of territory which was not 'effectively' occupied; but evidently the phrase 'effective occupation' can be very laxly interpreted. It provided that there should be free navigation of the Congo and Niger rivers, and freedom of trade for alienations within the Congo valley and certain other vaguely defined areas. But it made no similar provision for other parts of Africa; and it whittled away the value of what it did secure by the definite proviso that should parts of these areas be annexed by independent states, the restriction upon their control of trade should lapse. It recognised the illegality of the slave-trade, and imposed upon annexing powers the duty of helping to suppress it; this provision was made much fuller and more definite by a second conference at Brussels in 1890, on the demand of Britain, who had hitherto contended almost alone against the traffic in human flesh. But no attempt was made to define native rights, to safeguard native customs, to prohibit the maintenance of forces larger than would be necessary for the maintenance of order: in short, no attempt was made to lay down the doctrine that the function of a ruling power among backward peoples is that of a trustee on behalf of its simple subjects and on behalf of civilisation. That the partition of Africa should have been effected without open war, and that the questions decided at Berlin should have been so easily and peacefully agreed upon, seemed at the moment to be a good sign. But the spirit which the conference expressed was not a healthy spirit.

After 1884 the activity of the powers in exploration, annexation and development became more furious than ever. Britain now began seriously to arouse herself to the danger of exclusion from vast areas where her interests had hitherto been predominant; and it was during these years that all her main acquisitions of territory in Africa were made: Rhodesia and Central Africa in the south, East Africa and Somaliland in the East, Nigeria and the expansion of her lesser protectorates in the West. To these years also belonged the definite, and most unfortunate, emergence of Italy as a colonising power. She had got a foothold in Eritrea in 1883; in 1885 it was, with British aid, enlarged by the annexation of territory which had once been held by Egypt, but had been abandoned when she lost the Soudan. But the Italian claims in Eritrea brought on conflict with the neighbouring native power of Abyssinia. In spite of a sharp defeat at Dogali in 1887, she succeeded in holding her own in this conflict; and in 1889 Abyssinia accepted a treaty which Italy claimed to be a recognition of her suzerainty. But the Abyssinians repudiated this interpretation; and in a new war, which began in 1896, inflicted upon the Italians so disastrous a defeat at Adowa that they were constrained to admit the complete independence of Abyssinia—the sole native state which has so far been able to hold its own against the pressure of Europe. Meanwhile in

1889 and the following years Italy had, once more with the direct concurrence of Britain, marked out a new territory in Somaliland.

The main features of the years from 1884 to 1900 were the rapidity with which the territories earlier annexed were expanded and organised, more especially by France. In the 'nineties her dominions extended from the Mediterranean to the Guinea Coast, and she had conceived the ambition of extending them also across Africa from West to East. This ambition led her into a new and more acute conflict with Britain, who, having undertaken the reconquest of the Egyptian Soudan and the upper valley of the Nile, held that she could not permit a rival to occupy the upper waters of the great river, or any part of the territory that belonged to it. Hence when the intrepid explorer, Marchand, after a toilsome expedition which lasted for two years, planted the French flag at Fashoda in 1898, he was promptly disturbed by Kitchener, fresh from the overthrow of the Khalifa and the reconquest of Khartoum, and was compelled to withdraw. The tension was severe; no episode in the partition of Africa had brought the world so near to the outbreak of a European war. But in the end the dispute was settled by the Anglo-French agreement of 1898, which may be said to mark the conclusion of the process of partition. It was the last important treaty in a long series which filled the twenty years following 1878, and which had the result of leaving Africa, with the exception of Morocco, Tripoli, and Abyssinia, completely divided among the chief European states. Africa was the main field of the ambitions and rivalries of the European powers during this period; the other fields may be more rapidly surveyed. In Central Asia and the Near East the main features of the period were two. The first was the steady advance of Russia towards the south-east, which awakened acute alarms in Britain regarding India, and led to the adoption of a 'forward policy' among the frontier tribes in the north-west of India. The second was the gradual and silent penetration of Turkey by German influence. Here there was no partition or annexation, But Germany became the political protector of the Turk; undertook the reorganisation of his armies; obtained great commercial concessions; bought up his railways, ousting the earlier British and French concerns which had controlled them, and built new lines. The greatest of these was the vitally important project of the Bagdad railway, which was taken in hand just before the close of the period. It was a project whose political aims outweighed its commercial aims. And it provided a warning of the gigantic designs which Germany was beginning to work out. But as yet, in 1900, the magnitude of these designs was unperceived. And the problems of the Middle East were not yet very disturbing. The Turkish Empire remained intact; so did the Persian Empire, though both were becoming more helpless, partly owing to the decrepitude of their governments, partly owing to the pressure of European financial and trading interests. As yet the empires of the Middle East seemed to form a region comparatively free from European influence. But this was only seeming. The influence of Europe was at work in them; and it was probably inevitable that some degree of European political tutelage should follow as the only means of preventing the disintegration which must result from the pouring of new wine into the old bottles.

In the Far East—in the vast empire of China—this result seemed to be coming about inevitably and rapidly. The ancient pot-bound civilisation of China had withstood the impact of the West in the mid-nineteenth century without breaking down; but China had made no attempt, such as Japan had triumphantly carried out, to adapt herself to the new conditions, and her system was slowly crumbling under the influence of the European traders, teachers, and missionaries whom she had been compelled to admit. The first of the powers to take advantage of this situation was France, who already possessed a footing in Cochin-China, and was tempted during the colonial enthusiasm of the 'eighties to transform it into a general supremacy over Annam and Tonking. As early as 1874 she had obtained from the King of Annam a treaty which she interpreted as giving her suzerain powers. The King of Annam himself repudiated this interpretation, and maintained that he was a vassal of China. China took the same view; and after long negotiations a war between France and China broke out. It lasted for four years, and demanded a large expenditure of strength. But it ended (1885) with the formal recognition of French suzerainty over Annam, and a further decline of Chinese prestige.

Ten years later a still more striking proof of Chinese weakness was afforded by the rapid and complete defeat of the vast, ill-organised empire by Japan, the youngest of the great powers. The war gave to Japan Formosa and the Pescadores Islands, and added her to the list of imperialist powers. She would have won more still—the Liao-tang Peninsula and a sort of suzerainty over Korea—but that the European powers, startled by the signs of China's decay, and perhaps desiring a share of the plunder, intervened to forbid these annexations, on the pretext of defending the integrity of China. Russia, France and Germany combined in this step; Britain stood aloof. Japan, unwillingly giving way, and regarding Russia as the chief cause of her humiliation, began to prepare herself for a coming conflict. As for unhappy China, she was soon to learn how much sincerity there was in the zeal of Europe for the maintenance of her integrity. In 1896 she was compelled to permit Russia to build a railway across Manchuria; and to grant to France a 'rectification of frontiers' on the south, and the right of building a railway through the province of Yunnan, which lies next to Tonking. The partition of China seemed to be at hand. Britain and America vainly urged upon the other powers that China should be left free to direct her own affairs subject to the maintenance of 'the open door' for European trade. The other powers refused to listen, and in 1897 the beginning of the end seemed to have come. Germany, seizing on the pretext afforded by the murder of two German missionaries, stretched forth her 'mailed fist,' and seized the strong place and admirable harbour of Kiao-chau, the most valuable strategic position on the Chinese coast. That she meant to use it as a base for future expansion was shown by her lavish expenditure upon its equipment and fortification. Russia responded by seizing the strong place of Port Arthur and the Liao-Tang Peninsula, while every day her hold upon the great province of Manchuria was strengthened. Foreseeing a coming conflict in which her immense trading interests would be imperilled, Britain acquired a naval base on the Chinese coast by leasing Wei-hai-Wei. Thus all the European rivals were clustered round the decaying body of China; and in the last years of the century were already beginning to claim 'spheres of influence,' despite the protests of Britain and America. But the outburst of the Boxer Rising in 1900 — caused mainly by resentment of foreign intervention — had the effect of postponing the rush for Chinese territory. And when Britain and Japan made an alliance in 1902 on the basis of guaranteeing the status quo in the East, the overwhelming naval strength of the two allies made a European partition of China impracticable; and China was once more given a breathing-space. Only Russia could attack the Chinese Empire by land; and the severe defeat which she suffered at the hands of Japan in 1904-5 removed that danger also. The Far East was left with a chance of maintaining its independence, and of voluntarily adapting itself to the needs of a new age.

The last region in which territories remained available for European annexation consisted of the innumerable archipelagoes of the Pacific Ocean. Here the preponderant influence had been in the hands of Britain ever since the days of Captain Cook. She had made some annexations during the first three quarters of the century, but had on the whole steadfastly refused the requests of many of the island peoples to be taken under her protection. France had, as we have seen, acquired New Caledonia and the Marquesas Islands during the previous period, but her activity in this region was never very great. The only other European power in possession of Pacific territories was Spain, who held the great archipelago of the Philippines, and claimed also the numerous minute islands (nearly six hundred in number) which are known as Micronesia. When the colonial enthusiasm of the 'eighties began, Germany saw a fruitful field in the Pacific, and annexed the Bismarck Archipelago and the north-eastern quarter of New Guinea. Under pressure from Australia, who feared to see so formidable a neighbour established so near her coastline, Britain annexed the south-eastern quarter of that huge island. During the 'nineties the partition of the Pacific Islands was completed; the chief participators being Germany, Britain, and the United States of America.

The entry of America into the race for imperial possessions in its last phase was too striking an event to pass without comment. America annexed Hawaii in 1898, and divided the Samoan group with Germany in 1899. But her most notable departure from her traditional policy of self-imposed isolation from world-politics came when in 1898 she was drawn by the Cuban question into a war with Spain. Its result was the disappearance of the last relics of the Spanish Empire in the New World and in the Pacific. Cuba became an independent republic. Porto Rico was annexed by America. In the Pacific the Micronesian possessions of Spain were acquired by Germany. Germany would fain have annexed also the Philippine Islands. But America resolved herself to assume the task of organising and governing these rich lands; and in doing so made a grave breach with her traditions. Her new possession necessarily drew her into closer relations with the problems of the Far East; it gave her also some acquaintance with the difficulty of introducing Western methods among a backward people. During these years of universal imperialist excitement the spirit of imperialism seemed to have captured America as it had captured the European states; and this was expressed in a new interpretation of the Monroe doctrine, put forth by the Secretary of State during the Venezuela controversy of 1895. 'The United States,' said Mr. Olney, 'is practically sovereign on this continent (meaning both North and South America), 'and its fiat is law upon the subjects to which it confines its interposition.' No such gigantic imperial claim had ever been put forward by any European state; and it constituted an almost defiant challenge to the imperialist powers of Europe. It may safely be said that this dictum did not represent the settled judgment of the American people. But it did appear, in the last years of the century, as if the great republic were about to emerge from her self-imposed isolation, and to take her natural part in the task of planting the civilisation of the West throughout the world. Had she frankly done so, had she made it plain that she recognised the indissoluble unity and the common interests of the whole world, it is possible that her influence might have eased the troubles of the next period, and exercised a deterrent influence upon the forces of disturbance which were working towards the great catastrophe. But her traditions were too strong; and after the brief imperialist excitement of the 'nineties, she gradually relapsed once more into something like her old attitude of aloofness.

It is but a cursory and superficial view which we have been able to take of this extraordinary quarter of a century, during which almost the whole world was partitioned among a group of mighty empires, and the political and economic unity of the globe was finally and irrefragably established. Few regions had escaped the direct political control of European powers; and most of these few were insensibly falling under the influence of one or other of the powers: Turkey under that of Germany, Persia under that of Russia and Britain. No region of the earth remained exempt from the indirect influence of the European system. The civilisation of the West had completed the domination of the globe; and the interests of the great world-states were so intertwined and intermingled in every corner of the earth that the balance of power among them had become as precarious as was the European balance in the eighteenth century. The era of the world-states had very definitely opened. It remained to be seen in what spirit it was to be used, and whether it was to be of long duration. These two questions are one; for no system can last which is based upon injustice and the denial of right.

At this point we may well stop to survey the new world-states which had been created by this quarter of a century of eager competition.

First among them, in extent and importance, stood the new empire of France. It covered a total area of five million square miles, and in size ranked third in order, coming after the older empires of Russia and Britain. It had been the result of the strenuous labours of three-quarters of a century, dating from the first invasion of Algiers; it included also some surviving fragments of the earlier French Empire. But overwhelmingly the greater part of this vast dominion had been acquired during the short period which we have surveyed in this chapter; and its system of organisation and government had not yet had time to establish itself. It had been built only at the cost of strenuous labour, and many wars. Yet the French had shown in its administration that they still retained to the full that imaginative tact in the handling of alien peoples which had stood them in good stead in India and America during the eighteenth century. Once their rule was established the French had on the whole very little trouble with their subjects; and it is impossible to praise too highly the labours of civilisation which French administrators were achieving. So far as their subjects were concerned, they may justly be said to have regarded themselves as trustees. So far as the rest of the civilised world was concerned, the same praise cannot be given; for the French policy in the economic administration of colonies was definitely one of monopoly and exclusion. The French Empire fell into three main blocks. First, and most important, was the empire of Northern Africa, extending from Algiers to the mouth of the Congo, and from the Atlantic to the valley of the Nile. Next came the rich island of Madagascar; lastly the eastern empire of Annam and Tonking, the beginnings of which dated back to the eighteenth century. A few inconsiderable islands in the Pacific and the West Indies, acquired long since, a couple of towns in India, memories of the dreams of Dupleix, and the province of French Guiana in South America, which dated back to the seventeenth century, completed the list. For the most part a recent and rapid creation, it nevertheless had roots in the past, and was the work of a people experienced in the handling of backward races.

Next may be named the curious dominion of the Congo Free State, occupying the rich heart of the African continent. Nominally it belonged to no European power, but was a recognised neutral territory. In practice it was treated as the personal estate of the Belgian king, Leopold II. Subject to closer international restrictions than any other European domain in the non-European world, the Congo was nevertheless the field of some of the worst iniquities in the exploitation of defenceless natives that have ever disgraced the record of European imperialism. International regulations are no safeguard against misgovernment; the only real sanction is the character and spirit of the government. For the Congo iniquities Leopold II. must be held guilty at the bar of posterity. When he went to his judgment in 1908 this rich realm passed under the direct control of the Belgian government and parliament, and an immediate improvement resulted.

The least successful of the new world-states was that of Italy. Its story was a story of disaster and disappointment. It included some two hundred thousand square miles of territory; but they were hot and arid lands on the inhospitable shores of the Red Sea and in Somaliland. Italy had as yet no real opportunity of showing how she would deal with the responsibilities of empire.

The most remarkable, in many respects, of all these suddenly acquired empires was that of Germany. For it was practically all obtained within a period of three years, without fighting or even serious friction. It fell almost wholly within regions where Germany's interests had been previously negligible, and British trade predominant. Yet its growth had not been impeded, it had even been welcomed, by its rivals. This easily-won empire was indeed relatively small, being not much over one million square miles, little more than one-fifth of the French dominions. But it was five times as large as Germany itself, and it included territories which were, on the whole, richer than those of France. The comparative smallness of its area was due to the fact that Germany was actually the last to enter the race. She took no steps to acquire territory, she showed no desire to acquire it, before 1883; if she had chosen to begin ten years earlier, as she might easily have done, or if she had shown any marked activity in exploring or missionary work, without doubt she could have obtained a much larger share of African soil.

These rich lands afforded to their new masters useful supplies of raw materials, which were capable of almost indefinite expansion. They included, in East and South-West Africa, areas well suited for white settlement; but German emigrants, despite every encouragement, refused to settle in them.

An elaborately scientific system of administration, such as might be expected from the German bureaucracy, was devised for the colonies; officials and soldiers have from the beginning formed a larger proportion of their white population than in any other European possessions. Undoubtedly the government of the German colonies was in many respects extremely efficient. But over-administration, which has its defects even in an old and well-ordered country, is fatal to the development of a raw and new one. Although Germany has, in order to increase the prosperity of her colonies, encouraged foreign trade, and followed a far less exclusive policy than France, not one of her colonies, except the little West African district of Togoland, has ever paid its own expenses. In the first generation of its existence the German colonial empire, small though it is in comparison with the British or the French, actually cost the home government over 100,000,000 pounds in direct outlay.

The main cause of this was that from the first the Germans showed neither skill nor sympathy in the handling of their subject populations. The uniformed official, with his book of rules, only bewilders primitive folk, and arouses their resentment. But it was not only official pedantry which caused trouble with the subject peoples; still more it was the ruthless spirit of mere domination, and the total disregard of native rights, which were displayed by the German administration. The idea of trusteeship, which had gradually established itself among the rulers of the British dominions, and in the French colonies also, was totally lacking among the Germans. They ruled their primitive subjects with the brutal intolerance of Zabern, with the ruthless cruelty since displayed in occupied Belgium. This was what made the rise of the German dominion a terrible portent in the history of European imperialism. The spirit of mere domination, regardless of the rights of the conquered, had often shown itself in other European empires; but it had always had to struggle against another and better ideal, the ideal of trusteeship; and, as we have seen, the better ideal had, during the nineteenth century, definitely got the upper hand, especially in the British realms, whose experience had been longest. But the old and bad spirit reigned without check in the German realms. And even when, in 1907, it began to be seriously criticised, when its disastrous and unprofitable results began to be seen, the ground on which it was challenged in discussions in Germany was mainly the materialist ground that it did not pay.

The justification for these assertions is to be found in the history of the principal German colonies. In the Cameroons the native tribes, who had been so ready to receive European government that they had repeatedly asked for British protection, were driven to such incessant revolts that the annals of the colony seem to be annals of continuous bloodshed: forty-six punitive expeditions were chronicled in the seventeen years from 1891—long after the establishment of the German supremacy, which took place in

1884. The record of East Africa was even more terrible for the ferocity with which constant revolts were suppressed. But worst of all was the story of South-West Africa. There were endless wars against the various tribes; but they culminated in the hideous Herero war of 1903-6. The Hereros, driven to desperation by maltreatment, had revolted and killed some white farmers. They were punished by an almost complete annihilation. The spirit of this hideous slaughter is sufficiently expressed by the proclamation of the governor, General von Trotha, in 1904. 'The Herero people must now leave the land. Within the German frontier every Herero, with or without weapon, with or without cattle, will be shot. I shall take charge of no more women and children, but shall drive them back to their people, or let them be shot at.' Ten thousand of these unhappy people, mainly old men, women and children, were driven into the desert, where they perished. There is no such atrocious episode in the history of European imperialism since Pizarro's slaughter of the Incas; if even that can be compared with it.

The causes of these ceaseless and ruinous wars were to be found partly in the total disregard of native custom, and in the hide-bound pedantry with which German-made law and the Prussian system of regimentation were enforced upon the natives; but it was to be found still more in the assumption that the native had no rights as against his white lord. His land might be confiscated; his cattle driven away; even downright slavery was not unknown, not merely in the form of forced labour, which has been common in German colonies, but in the form of the actual sale and purchase of negroes. Herr Dernburg, who became Colonial Secretary in 1907, himself recorded that he met in East Africa a young farmer who told him that he had just bought a hundred and fifty negroes; he also described the settlers' pleasing practice of sitting beside the wells with revolvers, in order to prevent the natives from watering their cattle, and to force them to leave them behind; and he noted that officials nearly always carried negro whips with them. These practices, indeed, were condemned by the German Government itself, but only after many years, and mainly because they were wasteful. Government representatives have told the Reichstag, as Herr Schleitwein did in 1904, that they must pursue a 'healthy egoism,' and forswear 'humanitarianism and irrational sentimentality.' 'The Hereros must be forced to work, and to work without compensation and for their food only. ... The sentiments of Christianity and philanthropy with which the missionaries work must be repudiated with all energy.' This is what is called Realpolitik.

Is it too much to say that the appearance of the spirit thus expressed was a new thing in the history of European imperialism? Is it not plain that if this spirit should triumph, the ascendancy of Europe over the non-European world must prove to be, not a blessing, but an unmitigated curse? Yet the nation which had thus acquitted itself in the rich lands which it had so easily acquired was not satisfied; it desired a wider field for the exhibition of its Kultur, its conception of civilisation.

From the beginning it was evident that the colonial enthusiasts of Germany had no intention of resting satisfied with the considerable dominions they had won, but regarded them only as a beginning, as bases for future conquests. The colonies were not ends in themselves, but means for the acquisition of further power; and it was this, even more than the ruthlessness with which the subject peoples were treated, which made the growth of the German dominions a terrible portent. For since the whole world was now portioned out, new territories could only be acquired at the cost of Germany's neighbours. This was, indeed, at first the programme only of extremists; the mass of the German people, like Bismarck, took little interest in colonies. But the extremists proved that they could win over the government to their view; the German people, most docile of nations, could be gradually indoctrinated with it. And because this was so, because the ugly spirit of domination and of unbridled aggressiveness was in these years gradually mastering the ruling forces of a very powerful state, and leading them towards the catastrophe which was to prove the culmination of European imperialism, it is necessary to dwell, at what may seem disproportionate length, upon the development of German policy during the later years of our period.

Filled with pride in her own achievements, believing herself to be, beyond all rivalry, the greatest nation in the world, already the leader, and destined to be the controller, of civilisation, Germany could not bring herself to accept a second place in the imperial sphere. She had entered late into the field, by no fault of her own, and found all the most desirable regions of the earth already occupied. Now that 'world-power' had become the test of greatness among states, she could be content with nothing short of the first rank among world-states; if this rank could not be achieved, she seemed to be sentenced to the same sort of fate as had befallen Holland or Denmark: she might be ever so prosperous, as these little states were, but she would be dwarfed by the vast powers which surrounded her. But the German world-state was not to be the result of a gradual and natural growth, like the Russian, the British or the American world-states. The possibility of gradual growth was excluded by the fact that the whole world had been partitioned. Greatness in the non-European world must be, and might be, carved out in a single generation, as supremacy in Europe had been already attained, by the strong will, efficient organisation, and military might of the German government.

It was natural, perhaps inevitable, that a nation with the history of the German nation, with its ruling ideas, and with its apparently well-tried confidence in the power of its government to achieve its ends by force, should readily accept such a programme. The date at which this programme captured the government of Germany, and became the national policy, can be quite clearly fixed: it was in 1890, when Bismarck, the 'no colony man,' was driven from power, and the supreme direction of national affairs fell into the hands of the Emperor William II. An impressionable, domineering and magniloquent prince, inflated by the hereditary self-assurance of the Hohenzollerns, and sharing to the full the modern German belief in German superiority and in Germany's imperial destiny, William II. became the spokesman and leader of an almost insanely megalomaniac, but terribly formidable nation. During the first decade of his government the new ambitions of Germany were gradually formulated, and became more distinct. They were not yet very apparent to the rest of the world, in spite of the fact that they were expounded with vigour and emphasis in a multitude of pamphlets and books. The world was even ready to believe the Emperor's assertion that he was the friend of peace: he half believed it himself, because he would have been very ready to keep the peace if Germany's 'rights' could be attained without war. But many episodes, such as Kiao-Chau, and the Philippines, and the ceaseless warfare in the German colonies, and the restless enterprises of Pan-German intrigue, provided a commentary upon these pretensions which ought to have revealed the dangerous spirit which was conquering the German people.

It is difficult, in the midst of a war forced upon the world by German ambition, to take a sane and balanced view of the aims which German policy was setting before itself during these years of experiment and preparation. What did average German opinion mean by the phrase Weltmacht, world-power, which had become one of the commonplaces of its political discussions? We may safely assume that by the mass of men the implications of the term were never very clearly analysed; and that, if they had been analysable, the results of the analysis would have been widely different in 1890 and in 1914, except for a few fanatics and extremists. Was the world-power at which Germany was aiming a real supremacy over the whole world? In a vague way, no doubt, important bodies of opinion held that such a supremacy was the ultimate destiny of Germany in the more or less distant future; and the existence of such a belief, however undefined, is important because it helped to colour the attitude of the German mind towards more immediately practical problems of national policy. But as a programme to be immediately put into operation, world-power was not conceived in this sense by any but a few Pan-German fanatics; and even they would have recognised that of course other states, and even other world-powers, would certainly survive the most successful German war, though they would have to submit (for their own good) to Germany's will. Again, did the demand for world-power mean no more than that Germany must have extra-European territories, like Britain or

France? She already possessed such territories, though on a smaller scale than her rivals. Did the claim mean, then, that her dominions must be as extensive and populous as (say) those of Britain? Such an aim could only be obtained if she could succeed in overthrowing all her rivals, at once or in succession. And if she did that, she would then become, whatever her intentions, a world-power in the first and all-embracing sense. It is probably true that the German people, and even the extreme Pan-Germans, did not definitely or consciously aim at world-supremacy. But they had in the back of their minds the conviction that this was their ultimate destiny, and in aiming at 'world-power' in a narrower sense, they so defined their end as to make it impossible of achievement unless the complete mastery of Europe (which, as things are, means the mastery of most of the world) could be first attained. Certainly the ruling statesmen of Germany must have been aware of the implications of their doctrine of world-power. They were aware of it in 1914, when they deliberately struck for the mastery of Europe; they must have been aware of it in 1890, when they began to lay numerous plans and projects in all parts of the world, such as were bound to arouse the fears and suspicions of their rivals.

It is necessary to dwell for a little upon these plans and projects of the decade 1890-1900, because they illustrate the nature of the peril which was looming over an unconscious world. It would be an error to suppose that all these schemes were systematically and continuously pursued with the whole strength of the German state. They appealed to different bodies of opinion. Some of them were eagerly taken up for a time, and then allowed to fall into the background, though seldom wholly dropped. But taken as a whole they showed the existence of a restless and insatiable ambition without very clearly defined aims, and an eagerness to make use of every opening for the extension of power, which constituted a very dangerous frame of mind in a nation so strong, industrious, and persistent as the German nation.

In spite of the disappointing results of colonisation in Africa, the German colonial enthusiasts hoped that something suitably grandiose might yet be erected there: if the Belgian Congo could somehow be acquired, and if the Portuguese would agree to sell their large territories on the east and west coasts, a great empire of Tropical Africa might be brought into being. This vision has not been abandoned: it is the theme of many pamphlets published during the course of the war, and if Germany were to be able to impose her own terms, all the peoples of Central Africa might yet hope to have extended to them the blessings of German government as they have been displayed in the Cameroons and in the South-West.

In the 'nineties there seemed also to be hope in South Africa, where use might be made of the strained relations between Britain and the Boer

Republics. German South-West Africa formed a convenient base for operations in this region: it was equipped with a costly system of strategic railways, far more elaborate than the commerce of the colony required. There is no doubt that President Kruger was given reason to anticipate that he would receive German help: in 1895 (before the Jameson Raid) Kruger publicly proclaimed that the time had come 'to form ties of the closest friendship between Germany and the Transvaal, ties such as are natural between fathers and children'; in 1896 (after the Jameson Raid) came the Emperor's telegram congratulating President Kruger upon having repelled the invaders 'without recourse to the aid of friendly powers'; in 1897 a formal treaty of friendship and commerce was made between Germany and the Orange Free State, with which the Transvaal had just concluded a treaty of perpetual alliance. And meanwhile German munitions of war were pouring into the Transvaal through Delagoa Bay. But when the crisis came, Germany did nothing. She could not, because the British fleet stood in the way.

South America, again, offered a very promising field. There were many thousands of German settlers, especially in southern Brazil: the Pan-German League assiduously laboured to organise these settlers, and to fan their patriotic zeal, by means of schools, books, and newspapers. But the Monroe Doctrine stood in the way of South American annexations. Perhaps Germany might have been ready to see how far she could go with the United States, the least military of great powers. But there was good reason to suppose that the British fleet would have to be reckoned with; and a burglarious expedition to South America with that formidable watchdog at large and unmuzzled was an uninviting prospect.

In the Far East the prospects of immediate advance seemed more favourable, since the Chinese Empire appeared to be breaking up. The seizure of Kiao-chau in 1897 was a hopeful beginning. But the Anglo-Japanese alliance of 1902 formed a serious obstacle to any vigorous forward policy in this region. Once more the British fleet loomed up as a barrier.

Yet another dream, often referred to by the pamphleteers though never brought to overt action by the government, was the dream that the rich empire of the Dutch in the Malay Archipelago should be acquired by Germany. Holland herself, according to all the political ethnologists of the Pan-German League, ought to be part of the German Empire; and if so, her external dominions would follow the destiny of the ruling state. But this was a prospect to be talked about, not to be worked for openly. It would naturally follow from a successful European war.

A more immediately practicable field of operations was to be found in the Turkish Empire. It was here that the most systematic endeavours were made during this period: the Berlin-Bagdad scheme, which was to be the keystone of the arch of German world-power, had already taken shape before our period closed, though the rest of the world was strangely blind to its significance. Abstractly regarded, a German dominion over the wasted and misgoverned lands of the Turkish Empire would have meant a real advance of civilisation, and would have been no more unjustifiable than the British control of Egypt or India. This feeling perhaps explained the acquiescence with which the establishment of German influence in Turkey was accepted by most of the powers. They had yet to realise that it was not pursued as an end in itself, but as a means to further domination.

But neither the great Berlin-Bagdad project, nor any of the other dreams and visions, had been definitely put into operation during the decade 1890-1900. Germany was as yet feeling the way, preparing the ground, and building up her resources both military and industrial. Perhaps the main result which emerged from the tentative experiments of these years was that at every point the obstacle was the sprawling British Empire, and the too-powerful British fleet. The conviction grew that the overthrow of this fat and top-heavy colossus was the necessary preliminary to the creation of the German world-state.

This was a doctrine which had long been preached by the chief political mentor of modern Germany, Treitschke, who died in 1896. He was never tired of declaring that Britain was a decadent and degenerate state, that her empire was an unreal empire, and that it would collapse before the first serious attack. It would break up because it was not based upon force, because it lacked organisation, because it was a medley of disconnected and discordant fragments, worshipping an undisciplined freedom. That it should ever have come into being was one of the paradoxes of history; for it was manifestly not due to straightforward brute force, like the German Empire; and the modern German mind could not understand a state which did not rest upon power, but upon consent, which had not been built up, like Prussia, by the deliberate action of government, but which had grown almost at haphazard, through the spontaneous activity of free and self-governing citizens. Treitschke and his disciples could only explain the paradox by assuming that since it had not been created by force, it must have been created by low cunning; and they invented the theory that British statesmen had for centuries pursued an undeviating and Machiavellian policy of keeping the more virile states of Europe at cross-purposes with one another by means of the cunning device called the Balance of Power, while behind the backs of these tricked and childlike nations Britain was meanly snapping up all the most desirable regions of the earth. According to this view it was in some mysterious way Britain's fault that France and Germany were not the best of friends, and that Russia had been alienated from her ancient ally. But the day of reckoning would come when these mean devices would no longer avail, and the pampered, selfish, and overgrown colossus would find herself faced by hard-trained and finely tempered Germany, clad in her shining armour. Then, at the first shock, India would revolt; and the Dutch of South Africa would welcome their German liberators; and the great colonies, to which Britain had granted a degree of independence that no virile state would ever have permitted, would shake off the last shreds of subordination; and the ramshackle British Empire would fall to pieces; and Germany would emerge triumphant, free to pursue all her great schemes, and to create a lasting world-power, based upon Force and System and upon 'a healthy egoism,' not upon 'irrational sentimentalities' about freedom and justice.

These were the doctrines and calculations of Realpolitik. They were becoming more and more prevalent in the 'nineties. They seem definitely to have got the upper hand in the direction of national policy during the last years of the century, when Germany refused to consider the projects of disarmament put forward at the Hague in 1899, when the creation of the German navy was begun by the Navy Acts of 1898 and 1900, and when the Emperor announced that the future of Germany lay upon the water, and that hers must be the admiralty of the Atlantic. At the moment when the conquest of the world by European civilisation was almost complete, two conceptions of the meaning of empire, the conception of brutal domination pursued for its own sake, which has never been more clearly displayed than in the administration of the German colonies, and the conception of trusteeship, which had slowly emerged during the long development of the British Empire, stood forth already in sharp antithesis.

The dreadful anticipation of coming conflict weighed upon the world. France, still suffering from the wounds of 1870, was always aware of it. Russia, threatened by German policy in the Balkans, was more and more clearly realising it. But Britain was extraordinarily slow to awaken to the menace. As late as 1898 Mr. Joseph Chamberlain was advocating an alliance between Britain, Germany, and America to maintain the peace of the world; and Cecil Rhodes, when he devised his plan for turning Oxford into the training-ground of British youth from all the free nations of the empire, found a place in his scheme for German as well as for American students. The telegram to President Kruger in 1896 caused only a passing sensation. The first real illumination came with the extraordinary display of German venom against Britain during the South African war, and with the ominous doubling of the German naval programme adopted in the midst of that war, in 1900. But even this made no profound impression. The majority of the British people declined to believe that a 'great and friendly nation,' or its rulers, could deliberately enter upon a scheme of such unbridled ambition and of such unprovoked aggression.

VIII
THE BRITISH EMPIRE AMID THE WORLD-POWERS, 1878-1914

Throughout the period of rivalry for world-power which began in 1878 the British Empire had continued to grow in extent, and to undergo a steady change in its character and organisation.

In the partition of Africa, Britain, in spite of the already immense extent of her domains, obtained an astonishingly large share. The protectorates of British East Africa, Uganda, Nigeria, Nyasaland, and Somaliland gave her nearly 25,000,000 new negro subjects, and these, added to her older settlements of Sierra Leone and the Gold Coast, whose area was now extended, outnumbered the whole population of the French African empire. But besides these tropical territories she acquired control over two African regions so important that they deserve separate treatment: Egypt, on the one hand, and the various extensions of her South African territories on the other. When the partition of Africa was completed, the total share of Britain amounted to 3,500,000 square miles, with a population of over 50,000,000 souls, and it included the best regions of the continent: the British Empire, in Africa alone, was more than three times as large as the colonial empire of Germany, which was almost limited to Africa.

It may well be asked why an empire already so large should have taken also the giant's share of the last continent available for division among the powers of Europe. No doubt this was in part due to the sentiment of imperialism, which was stronger in Britain during this period than ever before. But there were other and more powerful causes. In the first place, during the period 1815-78 British influence and trade had been established in almost every part of Africa save the central ulterior, and no power had such definite relations with various native tribes, many of which desired to come under the protectorate of a power with whom the protection of native rights and customs was an established principle. In the second place, Britain was the only country which already possessed in Africa colonies inhabited by enterprising European settlers, and the activity of these settlers played a considerable part in the extension of the British African dominions. And in the third place, since the continental powers had adopted the policy of fiscal protection, the annexation of a region by any of them meant that the trade of other nations might be restricted or excluded; the annexation of a territory by Britain meant that it would be open freely and on equal terms to the trade of all nations. For this reason the trading interests in Britain, faced by the possibility of exclusion from large areas with which they had carried on traffic, were naturally anxious that as much territory as possible should be brought under British supremacy, in order that it might remain open to their trade.

It is the main justification for British annexations that they opened and developed new markets for all the world, instead of closing them; and it was this fact chiefly which made the acquisition of such vast areas tolerable to the other trading powers. The extension of the British Empire was thus actually a benefit to all the non-imperial states, especially to such active trading countries as Italy, Holland, Scandinavia, or America. If at any time Britain should reverse her traditional policy, and reserve for her own merchants the trade of the immense areas which have been brought under her control, nothing is more certain than that the world would protest, and protest with reason, against the exorbitant and disproportionate share which has fallen to her. Only so long as British control means the open door for all the world will the immense extent of these acquisitions continue to be accepted without protest by the rest of the world.

In the new protectorates of this period Britain found herself faced by a task with which she had never had to deal on so gigantic a scale, though she had a greater experience in it than any other nation: the task of governing justly whole populations of backward races, among whom white men could not permanently dwell, and whom they visited only for the purposes of commercial exploitation. The demands of industry for the raw materials of these countries involved the employment of labour on a very large scale; but the native disliked unfamiliar toil, and as his wants were very few, could easily earn enough to keep him in the idleness he loved. Slavery was the customary mode of getting uncongenial tasks performed in Africa; but against slavery European civilisation had set its face. Again, the ancient unvarying customs whereby the rights and duties of individual tribesmen were enforced, and the primitive societies held together, were often inconsistent with Western ideas, and tended to break down altogether on contact with Western industrial methods. How were the needs of industry to be reconciled with justice to the subject peoples? How were their customs to be reconciled with the legal ideas of their new masters? How were these simple folk to be taught the habits of labour? How were the resources of their land to be developed without interference with their rights of property and with the traditional usages arising from them? These were problems of extreme difficulty, which faced the rulers of all the new European empires. The attempt to solve them in a high-handed way, and with a view solely to the interests of the ruling race, led to many evils: it produced the atrocities of the Congo; it produced in the German colonies the practical revival of slavery, the total disregard of native customs, and the horrible sequence of wars and slaughters of which we have already spoken. In the British dominions a long tradition and a long experience saved the subject peoples from these iniquities. We dare not claim that there were no abuses in the British lands; but at least it can be claimed that government has always held it to be its duty to safeguard native rights, and to prevent the total break-up of the tribal system which could alone hold these communities together. The problem was not fully solved; perhaps it is insoluble. But at least the native populations were not driven to despair, and were generally able to feel that they were justly treated. 'Let me tell you,' a Herero is recorded to have written from British South Africa to his kinsmen under German rule, 'Let me tell you that the land of the English is a good land, since there is no ill-treatment. White and black stand on the same level. There is much work and much money, and your overseer does not beat you, or if he does he breaks the law and is punished.' There was a very striking contrast between the steady peace which has on the whole reigned in all the British dominions, and the incessant warfare which forms the history of the German colonies. The tradition of protection of native rights, established during the period 1815-78, and the experience then acquired, stood the British in good stead. During the ordeal of the Great War it has been noteworthy that there has been no serious revolt among these recently conquered subjects; and one of the most touching features of the war has been the eagerness of chiefs and their peoples to help the protecting power, and the innumerable humble gifts which they have spontaneously offered. Much remains to be done before a perfect solution is found for the problems of these dominions of yesterday. But it may justly be claimed that trusteeship, not domination, has been the spirit in which they have been administered; and that this is recognised by their subjects, despite all the mistakes and defects to which all human governments must be liable in dealing with a problem so complex.

Administrative problems of a yet more complex kind were raised in the two greatest acquisitions of territory made by Britain during these years, in Egypt and the Soudan, and in South Africa. The events connected with these two regions have aroused greater controversy than those connected with any other British dominions; the results of these events have been more striking, and in different ways more instructive as to the spirit and methods of British imperialism, than those displayed in almost any other field; and for these reasons we shall not hesitate to dwell upon them at some length.

The establishment of British control over Egypt was due to the most curious chain of unforeseen and unexpected events which even the records of the British Empire contain. Nominally a part of the Turkish Empire, Egypt had been in fact a practically independent state, paying only a small fixed tribute to the Sultan, ever since the remarkable Albanian adventurer, Mehemet Ali, had established himself as its Pasha in the confusion following the French occupation (1806). Mehemet Ali had been an extraordinarily enterprising prince. He had created a formidable army, had conquered the great desert province of the Soudan and founded its capital, Khartoum, and had nearly succeeded in overthrowing the Turkish Empire and establishing his own power in its stead: during the period 1825-40 he had played a leading role in European politics. Though quite illiterate, he had posed as the introducer of Western civilisation into Egypt; but his grandiose and expensive policy had imposed terrible burdens upon the fellahin (peasantry), and the heavy taxation which was necessary to maintain his armies and the spurious civilisation of his capital was only raised by cruel oppressions.

The tradition of lavish expenditure, met by grinding the peasantry, was accentuated by Mehemet's successors. It inevitably impoverished the country. Large loans were raised in the West, to meet increasing deficits; and the European creditors in course of time found it necessary to insist that specific revenues should be ear-marked as a security for their interest, and to claim powers of supervision over finance. The construction of the Suez Canal (opened 1869), which was due to the enterprise of the French, promised to bring increased prosperity to Egypt; but in the meanwhile it involved an immense outlay. At the beginning of our period Egypt was already on the verge of bankruptcy, and the Khedive was compelled to sell his holding of Suez Canal shares, which were shrewdly acquired for Britain by Disraeli.

But financial chaos was not the only evil from which Egypt suffered. There was administrative chaos also, and this was not diminished by the special jurisdictions which had been allowed to the various groups of Europeans settled in the country. The army, unpaid and undisciplined, was ready to revolt; and above all, the helpless mass of the peasantry were reduced to the last degree of penury, and exposed to the merciless and arbitrary severity of the officials, who fleeced them of their property under the lash. All the trading nations were affected by this state of anarchy in an important centre of trade; all the creditors of the Egyptian debt observed it with alarm. But the two powers most concerned were France and Britain, which between them held most of the debt, and conducted most of the foreign trade, of Egypt; while to Britain Egypt had become supremely important, since it now controlled the main avenue of approach to India.

When a successful military revolt, led by Arabi Pasha, threatened to complete the disorganisation of the country (1882), France and Britain decided that they ought to intervene to restore order, the other powers all agreeing. But at the last moment France withdrew, and the task was undertaken by Britain single-handed.[7] In a short campaign Arabi was overthrown; and now Britain had to address herself to the task of reconstructing the political and economic organisation of Egypt. It was her hope and intention that the work should be done as rapidly as possible, in order that she might be able to withdraw from a difficult and thankless task, which brought her into very delicate relations with the other powers interested in Egypt. But withdrawal was not easy. The task of reorganisation proved to be a much larger and more complicated one than had been anticipated; and it was greatly increased when the strange wave of religious fanaticism aroused by the preaching of the Mahdi swept over the Soudan, raised a great upheaval, and led to the destruction of the Egyptian armies of occupation. Britain had now to decide whether the revolting province should be reconquered or abandoned. Reconquest could not be effected by the utterly disorganised Egyptian army; if it was to be attempted, it must be by means of British troops. But this would not only mean a profitless expenditure, it would also indefinitely prolong the British occupation, which Britain was desirous of bringing to an end at the earliest possible moment.

[7] See above

The romantic hero, Gordon, was therefore sent to Khartoum to carry out the withdrawal from the Soudan of all the remaining Egyptian garrisons. On his arrival he came to the conclusion that the position was not untenable, and took no steps to evacuate. There was much dangerous delay and vacillation; and in the end Gordon was besieged in Khartoum, and killed by the bands of the Mahdi, before a relief force could reach him. But this triumph of Mahdism increased its menace to Egypt. The country could not be left to its own resources until this peril had been removed, or until the Egyptian army had been fully reorganised. So the occupation prolonged itself, year after year.

The situation was, in fact, utterly anomalous. Egypt was a province of Turkey, ruled by a semi-independent Khedive. Britain's chief agent in the country was in form only in the position of a diplomatic representative. But the very existence of the country depended upon the British army of occupation, and upon the work of the British officers who were reconstructing the Egyptian army. And its hope of future stability depended upon the work of the British administrators, financiers, jurists, and engineers who were labouring to set its affairs in order. These officials, with Sir Evelyn Baring (Lord Cromer) at their head, had an extraordinarily difficult task to perform. Their relations with the native government, which they constantly had to overrule, were difficult enough. But besides this, they had to deal with the agents of the other European powers, who, as representing the European creditors of the Egyptian debt, had the right to interfere in practically all financial questions, and could make any logical financial reorganisation, and any free use of the country's financial resources for the restoration of its prosperity, all but impossible.

Yet in the space of a very few years an amazing work of restoration and reorganisation was achieved. Financial stability was re-established, while at the same time taxation was reduced. The forced labour which had been exacted from the peasantry was abolished; they were no longer robbed of their property under the lash; they obtained a secure tenure in their land; and they found that its productive power was increased, by means of great schemes of irrigation. An impartial system of justice was organised — for the first time in all the long history of Egypt since the fall of the Roman Empire. The army was remodelled by British officers. Schools of lower and higher grade were established in large numbers. In short, Egypt began to assume the aspect of a prosperous and well-organised modern community. And all this was the work, in the main, of some fifteen years.

Meanwhile in the Soudan triumphant barbarism had produced an appalling state of things. It is impossible to exaggerate the hideousness of the regime of Mahdism. A ferocious tyranny terrorised and reduced to desolation the whole of the upper basin of the Nile; and the population is said to have shrunk from 12,000,000 to 2,000,000, although exact figures are of course unattainable. One of the evil consequences of this regime was that it prevented a scientific treatment of the flow of the Nile, on which the very life of Egypt depended. Scientific irrigation had already worked wonders in increasing the productivity of Egypt, but to complete this work, and to secure avoidance of the famines which follow any deficiency in the Nile-flow, it was necessary to deal with the upper waters of the great river. On this ground, and in order to remove the danger of a return of barbarism, which was threatened by frequent Mahdist attacks, and finally in order to rescue captives who were enduring terrible sufferings in the hands of the Mahdi, it appeared that the reconquest of the Soudan must be undertaken as the inevitable sequel to the reorganisation of Egypt. It was achieved, with a wonderful efficiency which made the name of Kitchener famous, in the campaigns of 1896-98. The reconquered province was nominally placed under the joint administration of Britain and Egypt; but in fact the very remarkable work of civilisation which was carried out in it during the years preceding the Great War was wholly directed by British agents and officers.

The occupation of the Soudan necessitated a prolongation of the British occupation of Egypt. But, indeed, such a prolongation was in any case inevitable; for the beneficial reforms in justice, administration, finance, and the organisation of the country's resources, which had been effected in half a generation, required to be carefully watched and nursed until they should be securely rooted: to a certainty they would have collapsed if the guardianship of Britain had been suddenly and completely withdrawn. The growing prosperity of Egypt, however, and still more the diffusion of Western education among its people, has naturally brought into existence a nationalist party, who resent what they feel to be a foreign dominance in their country, and aspire after the institutions of Western self-government. But it has to be noted that the classes among whom this movement has sprung up are not the classes who form the bulk of the population of Egypt—the fellahin, who from the time of the Pharaohs downwards have been exploited and oppressed by every successive conqueror who has imposed his rule on the country. This class, which has profited more than any other from the British regime, which has, under that regime, known for the first time justice, freedom from tyranny, and the opportunity of enjoying a fair share of the fruits of its own labour, is as yet unvocal. Accustomed through centuries to submission, accepting good or bad seasons, just or unjust masters, as the gods may send them, the fellah has not yet had time even to begin to have thoughts or opinions about his place in society and his right to a share in the control of his own destinies; and if the rule which has endeavoured to nurture him into prosperity and self-reliance were withdrawn, he would accept with blind submissiveness whatever might take its place. The classes among whom the nationalist movement finds its strength are the classes which have been in the past accustomed to enjoy some degree of domination; the relics of the conquering races, Arabs or Turks, who have succeeded one another in the rule of Egypt, the small traders and shopkeepers of the towns, drawn from many different races, the students who have been influenced by the knowledge and the political ideas of the West. It is natural and healthy that a desire to share in the government of their country should grow up among these classes: it is in some degree a proof that the influence of the regime under which they live has been stimulating. But it is also obvious that if these classes were at once to reassume, under parliamentary forms, the dominance which they wielded so disastrously until thirty years ago, the result must be unhappy. They are being, under British guidance, gradually introduced to a share in public affairs. But the establishment of a system of full self-government and national independence in Egypt, if it is to be successful, must wait until not only these classes, but also the classes beneath them, have been habituated to the sense of self-respect and of civic obligation by a longer acquaintance with the working of the Reign of Law.

Since the Great War broke out, the British position in Egypt has been regularised by the proclamation of a formal British protectorate. Perhaps the happiest fate which can befall the country is that it should make that gradual progress in political freedom, which is alone lasting, under the guidance of the power which has already given it prosperity, the ascendancy of an impartial law, freedom from arbitrary authority, freedom of speech and thought, and emancipation from the thraldom of foreign financial interests; and in the end it may possibly be the destiny of this ancient land, after so many vicissitudes, to take its place as one among a partnership of free nations in a world-encircling British Commonwealth of self-governing peoples.

The most vexed, difficult, and critical problems in the history of the British Empire since 1878—perhaps the most difficult in the whole course of its history—have been those connected with the South African colonies. In 1878 there were four distinct European provinces in South Africa, besides protected native areas, like Basutoland. All four had sprung from the original Anglo-Dutch colony of the Cape of Good Hope. In two of them—Cape Colony and Natal—the two European peoples, British and Dutch, dwelt side by side, the Dutch being in a majority in the former, the British in the latter; but in both the difficulty of their relationship was complicated by the presence of large coloured populations, which included not only the native African peoples, Hottentots, Kaffirs, Zulus, and so forth, but also a large number of Asiatics, Malays who had been brought in by the Dutch before the British conquest, and Indians who had begun to come in more recently in large numbers, especially to Natal. Difference of attitude towards these peoples between the British authorities and the Dutch settlers had been in the past, as we have seen, a main cause of friction between the two European peoples, and had caused the long postponement of full self-government. In the other two provinces, the Transvaal and the Orange Free State, the white inhabitants were, in 1878, almost exclusively Dutch. The native populations in these states were no longer in a state of formal slavery, but they were treated as definitely subject and inferior peoples: a law of the Transvaal laid it down that 'there shall be no equality in Church or State between white and black.' Thus the mutual distrust originally aroused by the native question still survived. It was intensified by ill-feeling between the Boers and British missionaries. When Livingstone, the British missionary hero, reported the difficulties which the Boers had put in his way, British opinion was made more hostile than ever. Of the two Boer republics, the Orange Free State had enjoyed complete independence since 1854; and no serious friction ever arose between it and the British government. But the Transvaal, which had been turbulent and restless from the first, had been annexed in 1878, largely because it seemed to be drifting into a war of extermination with the Zulus.

As a consequence, Britain was drawn into a badly managed Zulu-War; and when this dangerous tribe had been conquered, the Transvaal revolted. The Boers defeated a small British force at Majuba; whereupon, instead of pursuing the struggle, the British government resolved to try the effect of magnanimity, and conceded (1881 and 1884) full local independence to the Transvaal, subject only to a vague recognition of British suzerainty.

This was the beginning of many ills. The Transvaal Boers, knowing little of the world, thought they had defeated Britain; and under the lead of Paul Kruger, a shrewd old farmer who henceforth directed their policy with all but autocratic power, began to pursue the aim of creating a purely Dutch South Africa, and of driving the British into the sea. Kruger's policy was one of pure racial dominance, not of equality of rights. It was a natural aim, under all the conditions. But it was the source of grave evils. Inevitably it stimulated a parallel movement in Cape Colony, where Dutch and British were learning to live peaceably together. The Boer extremists also began to look about for allies, and were tempted to hope for aid from Germany, who had just established herself in South-West Africa. Full of pride, the Transvaalers, though they already held a great and rich country which was very thinly peopled, began to push outwards, and especially to threaten the native tribes in the barren region of Bechuanaland, which lay between the Transvaal and the German territory. To this Britain replied by establishing a protectorate over Bechuanaland (1884) at the request of native chiefs: the motive of this annexation was, not suspicion of Germany, for this suspicion did not yet exist, but the desire to protect the native population.

Kruger's vague project of a Dutch South Africa would probably have caused little anxiety so long as his resources were limited to the strength of the thinly scattered Boer farmers. But the situation was fundamentally altered by the discovery of immense deposits first of diamonds and then of gold in South Africa, and most richly of all in the Rand district of the Transvaal. These discoveries brought a rapid inrush of European miners, financiers, and their miscellaneous camp-followers, and in a few years a very rich and populous European community had established itself in the Transvaal, and had created as its centre the mushroom new city of Johannesburg (founded 1884). These immigrants, who came from many countries, but especially from Britain, changed the situation in the Transvaal; it seemed as though the majority among the white men in that state would soon be British.

A simple and primitive organisation of government, such as sufficed for the needs of Boer farmers, was manifestly inadequate for the needs of the new population, which included, in the nature of things, many undesirable elements; and it was natural that the mining population should desire to be brought under a more modern type of government, or to obtain an effective share in the control of their own affairs. But this was precisely what the Boers of Kruger's way of thinking were determined to refuse them. They were resolved that Boer ascendancy in the Transvaal should not be weakened. They therefore denied to the new immigrants all the rights of citizenship, and would not even permit them to manage the local affairs of Johannesburg. At the same time Kruger imposed heavy taxation upon the gold industry and the people who conducted it; and out of the proceeds he was able not only to pay the expenses of government without burdening the Boer farmers, but to build up the military power by means of which he hoped ultimately to carry out his great project. Thus the 'Uitlanders' found themselves treated as an inferior race in the land which their industry was enriching. They practically paid the cost of the government, but had no share in directing it.

The policy of racial ascendancy has seldom been pursued in a more mischievous or dangerous form. One cannot but feel a certain sympathy with the Boers' desire to maintain Boer ascendancy in the land which they had conquered. Yet it must be remembered that they were themselves very recent immigrants: the whole settlement of the Transvaal had taken place in Paul Kruger's lifetime.

The diamonds and the gold of the recent discoveries had produced in South Africa a new element of power: the power of great wealth, wielded by a small number of men. Some of these were, of course, mean and sordid souls, to whom wealth was an end in itself. But among them one emerged who was more than a millionaire, who was capable of dreaming great dreams, and had acquired his wealth chiefly in order that he might have the power to realise them. This was Cecil Rhodes, an almost unique combination of the financier and the idealist. If he was sometimes tempted to resort to the questionable devices that high finance seems to cultivate, and if his ideals took on sometimes a rather vulgar colour, reflected from his money-bags, nevertheless ideals were the real governing factors in his life.

He dreamed of a great united state of South Africa; it was to be a British South Africa; but it was to be British, not in the sense in which Kruger wished it to be Dutch, but in the sense that equality of treatment between the white races should exist within it, as in all the British lands. He dreamed also of a great brotherhood of British communities, or communities governed by British ideals, girdling the world, perhaps dominating it (for Rhodes was inclined to be a chauvinist), and leading it to peace and liberty. As a lad fresh from Oxford, in long journeyings over the African veldt, he had in a curious, childlike way thought out a theology, a system of politics, and a mode of life for himself; having reached the conclusion that the British race had on the whole more capacity for leading the world successfully than any other, he had resolved that it should be his life's business to forward and increase the influence of British ideas and of British modes of life; and he had systematically built up a colossal fortune in order that he might have the means to do this work. At the roots of this strange medley of poetry and chauvinism which filled his mind was an unchanging and deep veneration for the outstanding memory of his youth, Oxford, which in his mind stood for all the august venerable past of England, and was the expression of her moral essence. When he died, after a life of money-making and intrigue, in a remote and half-developed colony, it was found that most of his immense fortune had been left either to enrich the college where he had spent a short time as a lad, or to bring picked youths from all the British lands, and from what he regarded as the two great sister communities of America and Germany, so that they might drink in the spirit of England, at Oxford, its sanctuary.

His immediate task lay in South Africa, where, from the moment of his entry upon public life, he became the leader of the British cause as Kruger was the leader of the Dutch: millionaire-dreamer and shrewd, obstinate farmer, they form a strange contrast. The one stood for South African unity based upon equality of the white races: the other also for unity, but for unity based upon the ascendancy of one of the white races. In the politics of Cape Colony Rhodes achieved a remarkable success: he made friends with the Dutch party and its leader Hofmeyr, who for a long time gave steady support to his schemes and maintained him in the premiership. It was a good beginning for the policy of racial co-operation. But Rhodes's most remarkable achievement was the acquisition of the fertile upland regions of Mashonaland and Matabililand, now called Rhodesia in his honour. There were episodes which smelt of the shady practices of high finance in the events which led up to this acquisition. But in the result its settlement was well organised, after some initial difficulties, by the Chartered Company which Rhodes formed for the purpose. Now one important result of the acquisition of Rhodesia was that it hemmed in the Transvaal on the north; and, joined with the earlier annexation of Bechuanaland, isolated and insulated the two Dutch republics, which were now surrounded, everywhere except on the east, by British territory. From Cape Town up through Bechuanaland and through the new territories Rhodes drove a long railway line. It was a business enterprise, but for him it was also a great imaginative conception, a link of empire, and he dreamed of the day when it should be continued to join the line which was being pushed up the Nile from Cairo through the hot sands of the Soudan.

But Rhodes's final and most unhappy venture was the attempt to force, by violent means, a solution of the Transvaal problem. He hoped that the Uitlanders might be able, by a revolution, to overthrow Kruger's government, and, perhaps in conjunction with the more moderate Boers, to set up a system of equal treatment which would make co-operation with the other British colonies easy, and possibly bring about a federation of the whole group of South African States. He was too impatient to let the situation mature quietly. He forced the issue by encouraging the foolish Jameson Raid of 1895. This, like all wilful resorts to violence, only made things worse. It alienated and angered the more moderate Boers in the Transvaal, who were not without sympathy with the Uitlanders. It aroused the indignation of the Cape Colony Boers, and embittered racial feeling there. It put the British cause in the wrong in the eyes of the whole world, and made the Boers appear as a gallant little people struggling in the folds of a merciless python-empire. It increased immensely the difficulty of the British government in negotiating with the Transvaal for better treatment of the Uitlanders. It stiffened the backs of Kruger and his party. The German Kaiser telegraphed his congratulations on the defeat of the Raid 'without the aid of friendly powers,' and the implication that this aid would be forthcoming in case of necessity led the Boers to believe that they could count on German help in a struggle with Britain. So every concession to the Uitlanders was obstinately refused; and after three years more of fruitless negotiation, during which German munitions were pouring into the Transvaal, the South African War began. It may be that the war could have been avoided by the exercise of patience. It may be that the imperialist spirit, which was very strong in Britain at that period, led to the adoption of a needlessly high-handed tone. But it was neither greed nor tyranny on Britain's part which brought about the conflict, but simply the demand for equal rights.

The war was one in which all the appearances were against Britain, and the whole world condemned British greed and aggression. It was a case of Goliath fighting David, the biggest empire in the world attacking two tiny republics; yet the weaker side is not necessarily always in the right. It seemed to be a conflict for the possession of gold-mines; yet Britain has never made, and never hoped to make, a penny of profit out of these mines, which remained after the war in the same hands as before it. It was a case of the interests of financiers and gold-hunters against those of simple and honest farmers; yet even financiers have rights, and even farmers can be unjust. In reality the issue was a quite simple and straightforward one. It was the issue of racial ascendancy against racial equality, and as her traditions bade her, Britain strove for racial equality. It was the issue of self-government for the whole community as against the entrenched dominion of one section; and there was no question on which side the history of Britain must lead her to range herself. Whatever the rest of the world might say, the great self-governing colonies, which were free to help or not as they thought fit, had no doubts at all. They all sent contingents to take part in the war, because they knew it to be a war for principles fundamental to themselves.

The war dragged its weary course, and the Boers fought with such heroism, and often with such chivalry, as to win the cordial respect and admiration of their enemies. It is always a pity when men fight; but sometimes a fight lets bad blood escape, and makes friendship easier between foes who have learnt mutual respect. Four years after the peace which added the Transvaal and the Orange Free State as conquered dominions to the British Empire, the British government established in both of these provinces the full institutions of responsible self-government. As in Canada sixty years earlier, the two races were bidden to work together and make the best of one another; because now their destinies were freely under their own control. Yet this was even a bolder experiment than that of Canada, and showed a more venturesome confidence in the healing power of self-government. How has it turned out? Within five years more, the four divided provinces which had presented such vexed problems in 1878, were combined in the federal Union of South Africa, governed by institutions which reproduced those of Britain and her colonies.

In handing over to the now united states of South Africa the unqualified control of their own affairs, Britain necessarily left to them the vexed problem of devising a just relation between the ruling races and their subjects of backward or alien stocks; the problem which had been the source of most of the difficulties of South Africa for a century past, and which had long delayed the concession of full self-government. Nowhere in the world does this problem assume a more acute form than in South Africa, where there is not only a majority of negroes, mostly of the vigorous Bantu stock, but also a large number of immigrants mainly from India, who as subjects of the British crown naturally claim special rights. South Africa has to find her own solution for this complex problem; and she has not yet fully found it. But in two ways her association with the British Empire has helped, and will help, her to find her way towards it. If the earlier policy of the British government, guided by the missionaries, laid too exclusive an emphasis upon native rights, and in various ways hampered the development of the colony by the way in which it interpreted these rights, at least it had established a tradition hostile to that policy of mere ruthless exploitation of which such an ugly illustration was being given in German South-West Africa. An absolute parity of treatment between white and black must be not only impracticable, but harmful to both sides. But between the two extremes of a visionary equality and a white ascendancy ruthlessly employed for exploitation, a third term is possible—the just tutelage of the white man over the black, with a reasonable freedom for native custom. 'A practice has grown up in South Africa,' says the greatest of South African statesmen,[7] 'of creating parallel institutions, giving the natives their own separate institutions on parallel lines with institutions for whites. It may be that on these lines we may yet be able to solve a problem which may otherwise be insoluble.' It is a solution which owes much to the British experiments of the previous period; and the principle which inspires it was incorporated in the Act of Union. This is one of the innumerable fruitful experiments in government in which the British system is so prolific. Again, the problem of the relationship between Indian immigrants and white colonists is an acutely difficult one. It cannot be said to have been solved. But at least the fact that the South African Union and the Indian Empire are both partners in the same British commonwealth improves the chances of a just solution. It helped to find at least a temporary adjustment in 1914; in the future also it may contribute, in this as in many other ways, to ensure that a fair consideration is given to both sides of the thorny question of inter-racial relationship.

[7] General Smuts, May 22, 1917.

The events which led up to, and still more the events which followed, the South African War had thus brought a solution for the South African problem, which had been a continuous vexation since the moment of the British conquest. It was solved by the British panacea of self-government and equal rights. Who could have anticipated, twenty years or fifty years ago, the part which has been played by South Africa in the Great War? Is there any parallel to these events, which showed the gallant general of the Boer forces playing the part of prime minister in a united South Africa, crushing with Boer forces a revolt stirred up among the more ignorant Boers by German intrigue, and then leading an army, half Boer and half British, to the conquest of German South-West Africa?

The South African War had proved to be the severest test which the modern British Empire had yet had to undergo. But it had emerged, not broken, as in 1782, but rejuvenated, purged of the baser elements which had alloyed its imperial spirit, and confirmed in its faith in the principles on which it was built. More than that, on the first occasion on which the essential principles or the power of the empire had been challenged in war, all the self-governing colonies had voluntarily borne their share. Apart from a small contingent sent from Australia to the Soudan in 1885, British colonies had never before—indeed, no European colony had ever before—sent men oversea to fight in a common cause: and this not because their immediate interests were threatened, but for the sake of an idea. For that reason the South African War marks an epoch not merely in the history of the British Empire, but of European imperialism as a whole.

The unity of sentiment and aim which was thus expressed had, however, been steadily growing throughout the period of European rivalry; and doubtless in the colonies, as in Britain, the new value attached to the imperial tie was due in a large degree to the very fact of the eagerness of the other European powers for extra-European possessions. Imperialist sentiment began to become a factor in British politics just about the beginning of this period: in 1878 the Imperial Federation Society was founded, and about the same time Disraeli, who had once spoken of the colonies as 'millstones around our necks,' was making himself the mouthpiece of the new imperialist spirit. To this wave of feeling a very notable contribution was made by Sir John Seeley's brilliant book, "The Expansion of England." Slight as it was, and containing no facts not already familiar, it gave a new perspective to the events of the last four centuries of British history, and made the growth of the Empire seem something not merely casual and incidental, but a vital and most significant part of the British achievement. Its defect was, perhaps, that it concentrated attention too exclusively upon the external aspects of the wonderful story, and dwelt too little upon its inner spirit, upon the force and influence of the instinct of self-government which has been the most potent factor in British history. The powerful impression which it created was deepened by other books, like Froude's "Oceana" and Sir Charles Dilke's "Greater Britain," the title of which alone was a proclamation and a prophecy. It was strengthened also by the wonderful imperial pageants, like nothing else ever witnessed in the world, which began with the two Jubilee celebrations of 1887 and 1897, and were continued in the funerals of Queen Victoria and Edward VII., the coronations of Edward VII. and George V., and the superb Durbars of Delhi. The imaginative appeal of such solemn representations of a world-scattered fellowship of peoples and nations and tongues must not be underestimated. At first there was perhaps a suggestion of blatancy, and of mere pride in dominion, in the way in which these celebrations were received; the graver note of Kipling's 'Recessional,' inspired by the Jubilee of 1897, was not unneeded. But after the strain and anxiety of the South African War, a different temper visibly emerged.

More important than the pageants were the conferences of imperial statesmen which arose out of them. The prime ministers of the great colonies began to deliberate in common with the statesmen of Britain; and the discussions, though at first quite informal and devoid of authority, have become more intimate and vital as time has passed: a beginning at least has been made in the common discussion of problems affecting the Empire as a whole. And alongside of, and in consequence of, all this, imperial questions have been treated with a new seriousness in the British parliament, and the offices which deal with them have ceased to be, as they once were, reserved for statesmen of the second rank. The new attitude was pointedly expressed when in 1895 Mr. Joseph Chamberlain, the most brilliant politician of his generation, who could have had almost any office he desired, deliberately chose the Colonial Office. His tenure of that office was not, perhaps, memorable for any far-reaching change in colonial policy, though he introduced some admirable improvements in the administration of the tropical colonies; but it was most assuredly memorable for the increased intensity of interest which he succeeded in arousing in imperial questions, both at home and in the colonies. The campaign which he initiated, after the South African War, for the institution of an Imperial Zollverein or a system of Colonial Preference was a failure, and indeed was probably a blunder, since it implied an attempt to return to that material basis of imperial unity which had formed the core of the old colonial system, and had led to the most unhappy results in regard to the American colonies. But at least it was an attempt to realise a fuller unity than had yet been achieved, and in its first form included an inspiring appeal to the British people to face sacrifices, should they be necessary, for that high end. Whether these ideas contribute to the ultimate solution of the imperial problem or not, it was at least a good thing that the question should be raised and discussed.

One further feature among the many developments of this era must not be left untouched. It is the rise of a definitely national spirit in the greater members of the Empire. To this a great encouragement has been given by the political unity which some of these communities have for the first time attained during these years. National sentiment in the Dominion of Canada was stimulated into existence by the Federation of 1867. The unification of Australia which was at length achieved in the Federation of 1900 did not indeed create, but it greatly strengthened, the rise of a similar spirit of Australian nationality. A national spirit in South Africa, merging in itself the hostile racial sentiments of Boer and Briton, may well prove to be the happiest result of the Union of South Africa. In India also a national spirit is coming to birth, bred among a deeply divided people by the political unity, the peace, and the equal laws, which have been the greatest gifts of British rule; its danger is that it may be too quick to imagine that the unity which makes nationhood can be created merely by means of resolutions declaring that it exists, but the desire to create it is an altogether healthy desire. On the surface it might appear that the rise of a national spirit in the great members of the Empire is a danger to the ideal of imperial unity; but that need not be so, and if it were so, the danger must be faced, since the national spirit is too valuable a force to be restricted. The sense of nationhood is the inevitable outcome of the freedom and co-operation which the British system everywhere encourages; to attempt to repress it lest it should endanger imperial unity would be as short-sighted as the old attempt to restrict the natural growth of self-government because it also seemed a danger to imperial unity. The essence of the British system is the free development of natural tendencies, and the encouragement of variety of types; and the future towards which the Empire seems to be tending is not that of a highly centralised and unified state, but that of a brotherhood of free nations, united by community of ideas and institutions, co-operating for many common ends, and above all for the common defence in case of need, but each freely following the natural trend of its own development.

That is the conception of empire, unlike any other ever entertained by men upon this planet, which was already shaping itself among the British communities when the terrible ordeal of the Great War came to test it, and to prove as not even the staunchest believer could have anticipated, that it was capable of standing the severest trial which men or institutions have ever had to undergo.

IX
THE GREAT CHALLENGE, 1900-1914

At the opening of the twentieth century the long process whereby the whole globe has been brought under the influence of European civilisation was practically completed; and there had emerged a group of gigantic empires, which in size far surpassed the ancient Empire of Rome; each resting upon, and drawing its strength from, a unified nation-state. In the hands of these empires the political destinies of the world seemed to rest, and the lesser nation-states appeared to be altogether overshadowed by them. Among the vast questions which fate was putting to humanity, there were none more momentous than these: On what principles, and in what spirit, were these nation-empires going to use the power which they had won over their vast and varied multitudes of subjects? What were to be their relations with one another? Were they to be relations of conflict, each striving to weaken or destroy its rivals in the hope of attaining a final world-supremacy? Or were they to be relations of co-operation in the development of civilisation, extending to the whole world those tentative but far from unsuccessful efforts after international co-operation which the European states had long been endeavouring to work out among themselves?[8] At first it seemed as if the second alternative might be adopted, for these were the days of the Hague Conferences; but the development of events during the first fourteen years of the century showed with increasing clearness that one of the new world-states was resolute to make a bid for world-supremacy, and the gradual maturing of this challenge, culminating in the Great War, constitutes the supreme interest of these years.

> [8] See the Essay on Internationalism
> (Nationalism and Internationalism).

The oldest, and (by the rough tests of area, population, and natural resources) by far the greatest of these new composite world-states, was the British Empire, which included 12,000,000 square miles, or one-quarter of the land-surface of the globe. It rested upon the wealth, vigour, and skill of a population of 45,000,000 in the homeland, to which might be added, but only by their own consent, the resources of five young daughter-nations, whose population only amounted to about 15,000,000. Thus it stood upon a rather narrow foundation. And while it was the greatest, it was also beyond comparison the most loosely organised of all these empires. It was rather a partnership of a multitude of states in every grade of civilisation than an organised and consolidated dominion. Five of its chief members were completely self-governing, and shared in the common burdens only by their own free will. All the remaining members were organised as distinct units, though subject to the general control of the home government. The resources of each unit were employed exclusively for the development of its own welfare. They paid no tribute; they were not required to provide any soldiers beyond the minimum needed for their own defence and the maintenance of internal order. This empire, in short, was not in any degree organised for military purposes. It possessed no great land-army, and was, therefore, incapable of threatening the existence of any of its rivals. It depended for its defence firstly upon its own admirable strategic distribution, since it was open to attack at singularly few points otherwise than from the sea; it depended mainly, for that reason, upon naval power, and secure command of the sea-roads by which its members were linked was absolutely vital to its existence. Only by sea-power (which is always weak in the offensive) could it threaten its neighbours or rivals; and its sea-power, during four centuries, had always, in war, been employed to resist the threatened domination of any single power, and had never, in time of peace, been employed to restrict the freedom of movement of any of the world's peoples. On the contrary, the Freedom of the Seas had been established by its victories, and dated from the date of its ascendancy. The life-blood of this empire was trade; its supreme interest was manifestly peace. The conception of the meaning of empire which had been developed by its history was not a conception of dominion for dominion's sake, or of the exploitation of subjects for the advantage of a master. On the contrary, it had come to mean (especially during the nineteenth century) a trust; a trust to be administered in the interests of the subjects primarily, and secondarily in the interests of the whole civilised world. That this is not the assertion of a theory or an ideal, but of a fact and a practice, is sufficiently demonstrated by two unquestionable facts: the first that the units which formed this empire were not only free from all tribute in money or men, but were not even required to make any contribution towards the upkeep of the fleet, upon which the safety of all depended; the second that every port and every market in this vast empire, so far as they were under the control of the central government, were thrown open as freely to the citizens of all other states as to its own. Finally, in this empire there had never been any attempt to impose a uniformity of method or even of laws upon the infinitely various societies which it included: it not merely permitted, it cultivated and admired, varieties of type, and to the maximum practicable degree believed in self-government. Because these were the principles upon which it was administered, the real strength of this empire was far greater than it appeared. But beyond question it was ill-prepared and ill-organised for war; desiring peace beyond all things, and having given internal peace to one-quarter of the earth's population, it was apt to be over-sanguine about the maintenance of peace. And if a great clash of empires should come, this was likely to tell against it.

The second oldest—perhaps it ought to be described as the oldest—of the world-empires, and the second largest in area, was the Russian Empire, which covered 8,500,000 square miles of territory. Its strength was that its vast domains formed a single continuous block, and that its population was far more homogeneous than that of its rivals, three out of four of its subjects being either of the Russian or of kindred Slavonic stock. Its weaknesses were that it was almost land-locked, nearly the whole of its immense coastline being either inaccessible, or ice-bound during half of the year; and that it had not adopted modern methods of government, being subject to a despotism, working through an inefficient, tyrannical, and corrupt bureaucracy. In the event of a European war it was further bound to suffer from the facts that its means of communication and its capacity for the movement of great armies were ill-developed; and that it was far behind all its rivals in the control of industrial machinery and applied science, upon which modern warfare depends, and without which the greatest wealth of man-power is ineffective. At the opening of the twentieth century Russia was still pursuing the policy of Eastward expansion at the expense of China, which the other Western powers had been compelled to abandon by the formation of the Anglo-Japanese alliance. Able to bring pressure upon China from the landward side, she was not deterred by the naval predominance which this alliance enjoyed, and she still hoped to control Manchuria, and to dominate the policy of China. But these aims brought her in conflict with Japan, who had been preparing for the conflict ever since 1895. The outcome of the war (1904), which ended in a disastrous Russian defeat, had the most profound influence upon the politics of the world. It led to an internal revolution in Russia. It showed that the feet of the colossus were of clay, and that her bureaucratic government was grossly corrupt and incompetent. It forbade Russia to take an effective part in the critical events of the following years, and notably disabled her from checking the progress of German and Austrian ascendancy in the Balkans. Above all it increased the self-confidence of Germany, and inspired her rulers with the dangerous conviction that the opposing forces with which they would have to deal in the expected contest for the mastery of Europe could be more easily overthrown than they had anticipated. To the Russian defeat must be mainly attributed the blustering insolence of German policy during the next ten years, and the boldness of the final challenge in 1914.

The third of the great empires was that of France, with 5,000,000 square miles of territory, mostly acquired in very recent years, but having roots in the past. It rested upon a home population of only 39,000,000, but these belonged to the most enlightened, the most inventive, and the most chivalrous stock in Christendom. As France had, a hundred years before, raised the standard of human rights among the European peoples, so she was now bringing law and justice and peace to the backward peoples of Africa and the East; and was finding in the pride of this achievement some consolation for the brutality with which she had been hurled from the leadership of Europe.

The fourth of the great empires was America, with some 3,000,000 square miles of territory, and a vague claim of suzerainty over the vast area of Central and South America. Her difficult task of welding into a nation masses of people of the most heterogeneous races had been made yet more difficult by the enormous flood of immigrants, mainly from the northern, eastern, and south-eastern parts of Europe, which had poured into her cities during the last generation: they proved to be in many ways more difficult to digest than their predecessors, and they tended, in a dangerous way, to live apart and to organise themselves as separate communities. The presence of these organised groups made it sometimes hard for America to maintain a quite clear and distinctive attitude in the discussions of the powers, most of which had, as it were, definite bodies of advocates among her citizens; and it was perhaps in part for this reason that she had tended to fall back again to that attitude of aloofness towards the affairs of the non-American world from which she seemed to have begun to depart in the later years of the last century. Although she had herself taken a hand in the imperialist activities of the 'nineties, the general attitude of her citizens towards the imperial controversies of Europe was one of contempt or undiscriminating condemnation. Her old tradition of isolation from the affairs of Europe was still very strong—still the dominating factor in her policy. She had not yet grasped (indeed, who, in any country, had?) the political consequences of the new era of world-economy into which we have passed. And therefore she could not see that the titanic conflict of Empires which was looming ahead was of an altogether different character from the old conflicts of the European states, that it was fundamentally a conflict of principles, a fight for existence between the ideal of self-government and the ideal of dominion, and that it must therefore involve, for good or ill, the fortunes of the whole globe. She watched the events which led up to the great agony with impartial and deliberate interest. Even when the war began she clung with obstinate faith to the belief that her tradition of aloofness might still be maintained. It is not surprising, when we consider how deep-rooted this tradition was, that it took two and a half years of carnage and horror to convert her from it. But it was inevitable that in the end her still more deeply rooted tradition of liberty should draw her into the conflict, and lead her at last to play her proper part in the attempt to shape a new world-order.

We cannot stop to analyse the minor world-states, Italy and Japan; both of which might have stood aside from the conflict, but that both realised its immense significance for themselves and for the world.

Last among the world-states, both in the date of its foundation and in the extent of its domains, was the empire of Germany, which covered considerably less than 1,500,000 square miles, but rested upon a home population of nearly 70,000,000, more docile, more industrious, and more highly organised than any other human society. The empire of Germany had been more easily and more rapidly acquired than any of the others, yet since its foundation it had known many troubles, because the hard and domineering spirit in which it was ruled did not know how to win the affections of its subjects. A parvenu among the great states—having only attained the dignity of nationhood in the mid-nineteenth century—Germany has shown none of that 'genius for equality' which is the secret of good manners and of friendship among nations as among individuals. Her conversation, at home and abroad, had the vulgar self-assertiveness of the parvenu, and turned always and wholly upon her own greatness. And her conduct has been the echo of her conversation. She has persuaded herself that she has a monopoly of power, of wisdom, and of knowledge, and deserves to rule the earth. Of the magnitude and far-reaching nature of her imperialist ambitions, we have said something in a previous chapter. She had as yet failed to realise any of these vaulting schemes, but she had not for that reason abandoned any of them, and she kept her clever and insidious preparations on foot in every region of the world upon which her acquisitive eyes had rested. But the exasperation of her steady failure to achieve the place in the world which she had marked out as her due had driven her rulers more and more definitely to contemplate, and prepared her people to uphold, a direct challenge to all her rivals. The object of this challenge was to win for Germany her due share in the non-European world, her 'place in the sun.' Her view of what that share must be was such that it could not be attained without the overthrow of all her European rivals, and this would bring with it the lordship of the world. It must be all or nothing. Though not quite realising this alternative, the mind of Germany was not afraid of it. She was in the mood to make a bold attempt, if need be, to grasp even the sceptre of world-supremacy. The world could not believe that any sane people could entertain such megalomaniac visions; not even the events of the decade 1904-14 were enough to bring conviction; it needed the tragedy and desolation of the war to prove at once their reality and their folly. For they were folly even if they could be momentarily realised. They sprang from the traditions of Prussia, which seemed to demonstrate that all things were possible to him who dared all, and scrupled nothing, and calculated his chances and his means with precision. By force and fraud the greatness of Prussia had been built; by force and fraud Prussia-Germany had become the leading state of Europe, feared by all her rivals and safe from all attack. Force and fraud appeared to be the determining factors in human affairs; even the philosophers of Germany devoted their powers to justifying and glorifying them. By force and fraud, aided by science, Germany should become the leader of the world, and perhaps its mistress. Never has the doctrine of power been proclaimed with more unflinching directness as the sole and sufficient motive for state action. There was practically no pretence that Germany desired to improve the condition of the lands she wished to possess, or that they were misgoverned, or that the existing German territories were threatened: what pretence there was, was invented after war began. The sole and sufficient reason put forward by the advocates of the policy which Germany was pursuing was that she wanted more power and larger dominions; and what she wanted she proposed to take.

On the surface it seemed mere madness for the least and latest of the great empires to challenge all the rest, just as it had once seemed madness for Frederick the Great, with his little state, to stand up against all but one of the great European powers. But Germany had calculated her chances, and knew that there were many things in her favour. She knew that in the last resort the strength of the world-states rested upon their European foundations, and here the inequality was much less. In a European struggle she could draw great advantage from her central geographical position, which she had improved to the highest extent by the construction of a great system of strategic railways. She could trust to her superbly organised military system, more perfect than that of any other state, just because no other state has ever regarded war as the final aim and the highest form of state action. She commanded unequalled resources in all the mechanical apparatus of war; she had spared no pains to build up her armament works, which had, indeed, supplied a great part of the world; she had developed all the scientific industries in such a way that their factories could be rapidly and easily turned to war purposes; and having given all her thoughts to the coming struggle as no other nation had done, she knew, better than any other, how largely it would turn upon these things. She counted securely upon winning an immense advantage from the fact that she would herself fix the date of war, and enter upon it with a sudden spring, fully prepared, against rivals who, clinging to the hope of peace, would be unready for the onset. She hoped to sow jealousies among her rivals; she trusted to catch them at a time when they were engrossed in their domestic concerns, and in this respect fate seemed to play into her hands, since at the moment which she had predetermined, Britain, France, and Russia were all distracted by domestic controversies. She trusted also to her reading of the minds and temper of her opponents; and here she went wildly astray, as must always be the fate of the nation or the man who is blinded by self-complacency and by contempt for others.

But, above all, she put her trust in a vast political combination which she had laboriously prepared during the years preceding the great conflict: the combination which we have learned to call Mittel-Europa. None of us realised to how great an extent this plan had been put in operation before the war began. Briefly it depended on the possibility of obtaining an intimate union with the Austro-Hungarian Empire, a control over the Turkish Empire, and a sufficient influence or control among the little Balkan states to ensure through communication. If the scheme could be carried out in full, it would involve the creation of a practically continuous empire stretching from the North Sea to the Persian Gulf, and embracing a total population of over 150,000,000. This would be a dominion worth acquiring for its own sake, since it would put Germany on a level with her rivals. But it would have the further advantage that it would hold a central position in relation to the other world-powers, corresponding to Germany's central position in relation to the other nation-states of Europe. Russia could be struck at along the whole length of her western and south-western frontier; the British Empire could be threatened in Egypt, the centre of its ocean lines of communication, and also from the Persian Gulf in the direction of India; the French Empire could be struck at the heart, in its European centre; and all without seriously laying open the attacking powers to the invasion of sea-power.

It was a bold and masterful scheme, and it was steadily pursued during the years before the war. Austro-Hungary was easily influenced. The ascendancy of her ruling races—nay, the very existence of her composite anti-national empire—was threatened by the nationalist movements among her subject-peoples, who, cruelly oppressed at home, were more and more beginning to turn towards their free brothers over the border, in Serbia and Rumania; and behind these loomed Russia, the traditional protector of the Slav peoples and of the Orthodox faith. Austro-Hungary, therefore, leant upon the support of Germany, and her dominant races would be very willing to join in a war which should remove the Russian menace and give them a chance of subjugating the Serbs. This latter aim suited the programme of Germany as well as it suited that of Austria, since the railways to Constantinople and Salonika ran through Serbia. Serbia, therefore, was doomed; she stood right in the path of the Juggernaut car.

The acquisition of influence in Turkey was also comparatively easy. Constantinople is a city where lavish corruption can work wonders. Moreover Turkey was, in the last years of the nineteenth century, in bad odour with Europe; and Germany was able to earn in 1897 the lasting gratitude of the infamous Sultan Abdul Hamid by standing between him and the other European powers, who were trying to interfere with his indulgence in the pastime of massacring the Armenians. Turkey had had many protectors among the European powers. She had never before had one so complaisant about the murder of Christians. From that date Germany was all-powerful in Turkey. The Turkish army was reorganised under her direction, and practically passed under her control. Most of the Turkish railways were acquired and managed by German companies. And presently the great scheme of the Bagdad railway began to be carried through. The Young Turk revolution in 1908 and the fall of Abdul Hamid gave, indeed, a shock to the German ascendancy; but only for a moment. The Young Turks were as amenable to corruption as their predecessors; and under the guidance of Enver Bey Turkey relapsed into German suzerainty. Thus the most important parts of the great scheme were in a fair way of success by 1910. One of the merits of this scheme was that as the Sultan of Turkey was the head of the Mahomedan religion, the German protectorate over Turkey gave a useful mode of appealing to the religious sentiments of Mahomedans everywhere. Twice over, in 1898 and in 1904, the Kaiser had declared that he was the protector of all Mahomedans throughout the world. Most of the Mahomedans were subjects either of Britain, France, or Russia—the three rival empires that were to be overthrown. As General Bernhardi put it, Germany in her struggle for Weltmacht must supplement her material weapons with spiritual weapons.

To obtain a similar ascendancy over the Balkan states was more difficult; for the Turk was the secular enemy of all of them, and Austria was the foe of two of the four, and to bring these little states into partnership with their natural enemies seemed an all but impossible task. Yet a good deal could be, and was, done. In two of the four chief Balkan states German princes occupied the thrones, a Hohenzollern in Rumania, a Coburger in Bulgaria; in a third, the heir-apparent to the Greek throne was honoured with the hand of the Kaiser's own sister. Western peoples had imagined that the day had gone by when the policy of states could be deflected by such facts; especially as the Balkan states all had democratic parliamentary constitutions. But the Germans knew better than the West. They knew that kings could still play a great part in countries where the bulk of the electorate were illiterate, and where most of the class of professional politicians were always open to bribes. Their calculations were justified. King Carol of Rumania actually signed a treaty of alliance with Germany without consulting his ministers or parliament. King Ferdinand of

Bulgaria was able to draw his subjects into an alliance with the Turks, who had massacred their fathers in 1876, against the Russians, who had saved them from destruction. King Constantine of Greece was able to humiliate and disgrace the country over which he ruled, in order to serve the purposes of his brother-in-law. These sovereigns may have been the unconscious implements of a policy which they did not understand. But they earned their wages.

There were, indeed, two moments when the great scheme came near being wrecked. One was when Italy, the sleeping partner of the Triple Alliance, who was not made a sharer in these grandiose and vile projects, attacked and conquered the Turkish province of Tripoli in 1911, and strained to breaking-point the loyalty of the Turks to Germany. The other was when, under the guidance of the two great statesmen of the Balkans, Venizelos of Greece and Pashitch of Serbia, the Balkan League was formed, and the power of Turkey in Europe broken. If the League had held together, the great German project would have been ruined, or at any rate gravely imperilled. But Germany and Austria contrived to throw an apple of discord among the Balkan allies at the Conference of London in 1912, and then stimulated Bulgaria to attack Serbia and Greece. The League was broken up irreparably; its members had been brought into a sound condition of mutual hatred; and Bulgaria, isolated among distrustful neighbours, was ready to become the tool of Germany in order that by her aid she might achieve (fond hope!) the hegemony of the Balkans. This brilliant stroke was effected in 1913—the year before the Great War. All that remained was to ruin Serbia. For that purpose Austria had long been straining at the leash. She had been on the point of making an attack in 1909, in 1912, in 1913. In 1914 the leash was slipped. If the rival empires chose to look on while Serbia was destroyed, well and good: in that case the Berlin-Bagdad project could be systematically developed and consolidated, and the attack on the rival empires could come later. If not, still it was well; for all was ready for the great challenge.

We have dwelt at some length upon this gigantic project, because it has formed during all these years the heart and centre of the German designs, and even to-day it is the dearest of German hopes. Not until she is utterly defeated will she abandon it; because its abandonment must involve the abandonment of every hope of a renewed attempt at world-supremacy, after an interval for reorganisation and recovery. Not until the German control over Austria and Turkey, more complete to-day, after two and a half years of war, than it has ever been before, has been destroyed by the splitting up of Austria among the nationalities to which her territory belongs, and by the final overthrow of the Turkish Empire, will the German dream of world-dominion be shattered.

But while this fundamentally important project was being worked out, other events, almost equally momentous in their bearing upon the coming conflict, were taking place elsewhere. It was the obvious policy of Germany to keep her rivals on bad terms with one another. The tradition of Bismarck bade her isolate each victim before it was destroyed. But the insolence and the megalomania of modern Germany made this difficult. German writers were busily and openly explaining the fate marked out for all the other powers. France was to be so crushed that she would 'never again be able to stand in our path.' The bloated and unconsolidated empire of Britain was to be shattered. The Russian barbarians were to be thrust back into Asia. And what the pamphleteers and journalists wrote was expressed with almost equal clearness in the tone of German diplomacy. In face of all this, the clumsy attempts of the German government to isolate their rivals met with small success, even though these rivals had many grounds of controversy among themselves. France knew what she had to fear; and the interpolation of a few clumsy bids for her favour amid the torrent of insults against her which filled the German press, were of no avail; especially as she had to look on at the unceasing petty persecution practised in the lost provinces of Alsace-Lorraine. Russia had been alienated by the first evidences of German designs in the Balkans, and driven into a close alliance with France. Britain, hitherto obstinately friendly to Germany, began to be perturbed by the growing German programmes of naval construction from 1900 onwards, by the absolute refusal of Germany to consider any proposal for mutual disarmament or retardation of construction, and above all by the repeated assertions of the head of the German state that Germany aspired to naval supremacy, that her future was on the sea, that the trident must be in her hands. Should the trident fall into any but British hands, the existence of the British Empire, and the very livelihood of the British homeland, would rest at the mercy of him who wielded it. So, quite inevitably, the three threatened empires drew together and reconciled their differences in the Franco-British agreement of 1904 and the Russo-British agreement of 1907.

These agreements dealt wholly with extra-European questions, and therefore deserve some analysis. In the Franco-British agreement the main feature was that while France withdrew her opposition to the British position in Egypt, Britain on her side recognised the paramount political interest of France in Morocco. It was the agreement about Morocco which counted for most; because it was the beginning of a controversy which lasted for seven years, which was twice used by Germany as a means for testing, and endeavouring to break, the friendship of her rivals, and which twice brought Europe to the verge of war.

Morocco is a part of that single region of mountainous North Africa of which France already controlled the remainder, Tunis and Algeria. Peoples of the same type inhabited the whole region, but while in Tunis and Algeria they were being brought under the influence of law and order, in Morocco they remained in anarchy. Only a conventional line divided Morocco from Algeria, and the anarchy among the tribesmen on one side of the line inevitably had an unhappy effect upon the people on the other side of the line. More than once France had been compelled, for the sake of Algeria, to intervene in Morocco. It is impossible to exaggerate the anarchy which existed in the interior of this rich and wasted country. It was, indeed, the most lawless region remaining in the world: when Mr. Bernard Shaw wished to find a scene for a play in which the hero should be a brigand chief leading a band of rascals and outlaws from all countries, Morocco presented the only possible scene remaining in the world. And this anarchy was the more unfortunate, not only because the country was naturally rich and ought to have been prosperous, but also because it lay in close proximity to great civilised states, and on one of the main routes of commerce at the entrance to the Mediterranean. In its ports a considerable traffic was carried on by European traders, but this traffic was, owing to the anarchic condition of the country, nothing like as great as it ought to have been. In 1905, 39 per cent. of it was controlled by French traders, 32 per cent. by British traders, 12 per cent. by German traders, and 5 per cent. by Spanish traders. Manifestly this was a region where law and order ought to be established, in the interests of civilisation. The powers most directly concerned were in the first place France, with her neighbouring territory and her preponderant trade; in the second place Britain, whose strategic interests as well as her trading interests were involved; in the third place Spain, which directly faced the Morocco coast; while Germany had only trading interests involved, and so long as these were safeguarded, had no ground of complaint. If any single power was to intervene, manifestly the first claim was upon France.

In 1900 France had directed the attention of Europe to the disorderly condition of Morocco, and had proposed to intervene to restore order, on the understanding that she should not annex the country, or interfere with the trading rights of other nations. Some states agreed; Germany made no reply, but made no objection. But owing to the opposition of Britain, who was then on bad terms with France and feared to see an unfriendly power controlling the entrance to the Mediterranean, no action was taken; and in the next years the chaos in Morocco grew worse. By the agreement of 1904 Britain withdrew her objection to French intervention, and recognised the prior political rights of France in Morocco, on the condition that the existing government of Morocco should be maintained, that none of its territory should be annexed, and that 'the open door' should be preserved for the trade of all nations. But, of course, it was possible, and even probable, that the existing Moroccan government could not be made efficient. In that case, what should happen? The possibility had to be contemplated by reasonable statesmen, and provided against. But to do so in a public treaty would have been to condemn beforehand the existing system. Therefore a hypothetical arrangement was made for this possible future event in a secret treaty, to which Spain was made a party; whereby it was provided that if the arrangement should break down, and France should have to establish a definite protectorate, the vital part of the north coast should pass under the control of Spain.

To the public part of these arrangements, which alone were of immediate importance, no objection was made by any of the other powers, and the German Chancellor told the Reichstag that German interests were not affected. France accordingly drew up a scheme of reforms in the government of Morocco, which the Sultan was invited to accept. But before he had accepted them the German Kaiser suddenly came to Tangier in his yacht, had an interview with the Sultan in which he urged him to reject the French demands, and made a public speech in which he declared himself the protector of the Mahomedans, asserted that no European power had special rights in Morocco, and announced his determination to support the 'independence and integrity' of Morocco—which in existing circumstances meant the maintenance of anarchy. What was the reason for this sudden and insolent intervention—made without any previous communication with France? The main reason was that France's ally, Russia, had just been severely defeated by Japan, and would not be able to take part in a European war. Therefore, it appeared, France might be bullied; Britain might not be willing to risk war on such an issue; the Entente of 1904 might be destroyed; the extension of French influence might be prevented; and the preservation of a state of anarchy in Morocco would leave open the chance of a seizure of that country by Germany at a later date, thus enabling her to dominate the entrance to the Mediterranean, and to threaten Algeria. But this pretty scheme did not succeed. The Entente held firm. Britain gave steady support to France, as indeed she was bound in honour to do; and in the end a conference of the powers was held at Algeciras (Spain). At this conference the predominating right of France to political influence in Morocco was formally recognised; and it was agreed that the government of the Sultan should be maintained, and that all countries should have equal trading rights in Morocco. This was, of course, the very basis of the Franco-British agreement. On every point at which she tried to score a success over France, Germany was defeated by the votes of the other powers, even her own ally, Italy, deserting her.

But the German intervention had had its effect. The Sultan had refused the French scheme of reform. The elements of disorder in Morocco were encouraged to believe that they had the protection of Germany, and the activity of German agents strengthened this belief. The anarchy grew steadily worse. In 1907 Sir Harry Maclean was captured by a brigand chief, and the British government had to pay 20,000 pounds ransom for his release. In the same year a number of European workmen engaged on harbour works at Casablanca were murdered by tribesmen; and the French had to send a force which had a year's fighting before it reduced the district to order. In 1911 the Sultan was besieged in his capital (where there were a number of European residents) by insurgent tribesmen, and had to invite the French to send an army to his relief.

This was seized upon by Germany as a pretext. Morocco was no longer 'independent.' The agreement of Algecras was dead. Therefore she resumed her right to put forward what claims she pleased in Morocco. Suddenly her gunboat, the Panther, appeared off Agadir. It was meant as an assertion that Germany had as much right to intervene in Morocco as France. And it was accompanied by a demand that if France wanted to be left free in Morocco, she must buy the approval of Germany. The settlement of Morocco was to be a question solely between France and Germany. The Entente of 1904, the agreement of 1906, the Moroccan interests of Britain (much more important than those of Germany), and the interests of the other powers of the Algeciras Conference, were to count for nothing. Germany's voice must be the determining factor. But Germany announced that she was willing to be bought off by large concessions of French territory elsewhere—provided that Britain was not allowed to have anything to say: provided, that is, that the agreement of 1904 was scrapped. This was a not too subtle way of trying to drive a wedge between two friendly powers. It did not succeed. Britain insisted upon being consulted. There was for a time a real danger of war. In the end peace was maintained by the cession by France of considerable areas in the Congo as the price of German abstention from intervening in a sphere where she had no right to intervene. But Morocco was left under a definite French protectorate.

We have dwelt upon the Morocco question at some length, partly because it attracted a vast amount of interest during the years of preparation for the war; partly because it affords an extraordinarily good illustration of the difficulty of maintaining peaceable relations with Germany, and of the spirit in which Germany approached the delicate questions of inter-imperial relationships—a spirit far removed indeed from that friendly willingness for compromise and co-operation by which alone the peace of the world could be maintained; and partly because it illustrates the crudity and brutality of the methods by which Germany endeavoured to separate her intended victims. It is improbable that she ever meant to go to war on the Moroccan question. She meant to go to war on whatever pretext might present itself when all her preparations were ready; but in the meanwhile she would avoid war on all questions but one: and that one was the great Berlin-Bagdad project, the keystone of her soaring arch of Empire. She would fight to prevent the ruin of that scheme. Otherwise she would preserve the peace, she would even make concessions to preserve the peace, until the right moment had come. In that sense Germany was a peace-loving power: in that sense alone.

On the agreement between Russia and Britain in 1907 it is unnecessary to dwell with such fulness. The agreement turned mainly upon the removal of causes of friction in the Middle East — in Persia and the Persian Gulf, and in Tibet. These were in themselves interesting and thorny questions, especially the question of Persia, where the two powers established distinct spheres of interest and a sort of joint protectorate. But they need not detain us, because they had no direct bearing upon the events leading up to the war, except in so far as, by removing friction between two rivals of long standing, they made it possible for them to co-operate for their common defence against a menace that became more and more apparent.

From 1907 onwards Germany found herself confronted by united defensive action on the part of the three empires whose downfall she intended to compass. It was not (except as regarded France and Russia) a formal alliance which bound these powers. There was no fixed agreement between them as to military co-operation. France and Britain had indeed, in 1906 and in 1911, consulted as to the military steps they should take if they were drawn into war, as seemed likely in those years, but neither was in any way bound to help the other under all circumstances. France and Britain had also agreed that the French fleet should be concentrated in the Mediterranean, the main British fleet in the North Sea. This arrangement (which was universally known, and, indeed, could not be concealed) put Britain under a moral obligation to defend France against naval attack, but only if France were the object of aggression. It was, therefore, actually a safeguard of peace, since it ensured that neither France nor, consequently, her ally, Russia, would begin a war without being sure of the concurrence of Britain, the most pacific of powers. As the diplomatic records show, at the opening of the Great War they were not sure of this concurrence, even for naval purposes, until August 1, when the die was already cast. The Triple Entente, therefore, was not an alliance; it was only an agreement for common diplomatic action in the hope of averting a terrible menace.

Until 1911 Germany, or some elements in Germany, seem to have hoped that she could get her own way by bullying and rattling her sabre, and that by these means she could frighten her rivals, make them mutually distrustful, and so break up their combination and deal with them in detail. Those who held this view were the peace-party (so-called), and they included the Kaiser and his Chancellor. They would probably not themselves have accepted this description of their policy, but in practice this is what it meant. But there was always a formidable and influential party in Germany which had no patience with these hesitations, and was eager to draw the sabre. It included the men of the General Staff, backed by the numerous Pan-German societies and newspapers. The issue of the Morocco question in 1911, which showed that the policy of bullying had failed, played into the hands of the men of violence; and from this moment began the last strenuous burst of military preparation which preceded the war. In 1911 was passed the first of a series of Army Acts for the increase of the already immense German army, and still more for the provision of vast equipment and the scientific apparatus of destruction; two further Acts for the same purpose followed in 1912 and in 1913. In 1911 also was published General Bernhardi's famous book, which defined and described the course of future action, and the aim which Germany was henceforth to pursue with all her strength: Weltmacht oder Niedergang, world-power or downfall.

The events in the Balkans in 1912 and 1913 completed the conversion of those who still clung to the policy of peaceful bullying. The formation and triumph of the Balkan League in 1912 formed a grave set-back for the Berlin-Bagdad project, which would be ruined if these little states became strong enough, or united enough, to be independent. The break-up of the Balkan League and the second Balkan War of 1913 improved the situation from the German point of view. But they left Serbia unsatisfactorily strong, and Serbia distrusted Austria, and controlled the communications with Constantinople. Serbia must be destroyed; otherwise the Berlin-Bagdad project, and with it the world-power of which it was to be the main pillar, would be always insecure. Austria was for attacking Serbia at once in 1913. Germany held her back: the widening of the Kiel Canal was not completed, and the fruits of the latest Army Acts were not yet fully reaped. But all was ready in 1914; and the Great Challenge was launched. It would have been launched at or about that time even if an unpopular Austrian archduke, significantly unguarded by the Austrian police, had NOT been most opportunely murdered by an Austrian subject on Austrian territory. The murder was only a pretext. The real cause of the war was the resolution of Germany to strike for world-supremacy, and her belief that the time was favourable for the great adventure.

Meanwhile, what had the threatened empires been doing during the years of strenuous German preparation which began in 1911? Their governments could not but be aware of the enormous activity which was taking place in that country — which was unthreatened on any side — though they probably did not know how thorough and how elaborate it was. What steps did they take to guard against the danger? Russia was busy constructing strategic railways, to make the movement of troops easier; she was erecting new munition factories. But neither could be quickly got ready. France imposed upon the whole of her manhood the obligation of serving for three instead of for two years in the army. Britain reorganised her small professional army, created the Territorial Force, and began the training of a large officer class in all the universities and public schools. But she did not attempt to create a national army. If she had done so, this would have been a signal for the precipitation of the war. Besides, Britain obstinately clung to the belief that so monstrous a crime as Germany seemed to be contemplating could never be committed by a civilised nation; and she trusted mainly to her fleet for her own security.

But Britain unquestionably laboured with all her might to conjure away the nightmare. From 1906 onwards she had made, in vain, repeated attempts to persuade Germany to accept a mutual disarmament or retardation of naval construction. In 1912 she resolved upon a more definite step. The German newspapers were full of talk about the British policy of 'encircling' Germany in order to attack and destroy her, which they attributed mainly to Sir Edward Grey. It was a manifest absurdity, since the Franco-Russian alliance was formed in 1894, at a time when Britain was on bad terms with both France and Russia, and the agreements later made with these two countries were wholly devoted to removing old causes of dispute between them. But the German people obviously believed it. Perhaps the German government also believed it? Britain resolved to remove this apprehension. Accordingly in 1912 Lord Haldane was sent to Germany with a formal and definite statement, authorised by the Cabinet, to the effect that Britain had made no alliance or understanding which was aimed against Germany, and had no intention of doing so. That being so, since Germany need have no fear of an attack from Britain, why should not the two powers agree to reduce their naval expenditure? The German reply was that to stop the naval programme was impossible, but that construction might be DELAYED, on one condition— that both powers should sign a formal agreement drawn up by Germany. Each power was to pledge itself to absolute neutrality in any European war in which the other was engaged. Each power was to undertake to make no new alliances. But this agreement was not to affect existing alliances or the duties arising under them. This proposal was an obvious trap, and the German ministers who proposed it must have had the poorest opinion of the intelligence of English statesmen if they thought it was likely to be accepted. For observe that it left Germany, in conjunction with Austria, free to attack France and Russia. It left the formidable Triple Alliance unimpaired. But it tied the hands of Britain, who had no existing European alliances, enforced neutrality upon her in such a war, and compelled her to look on idly and wait her turn. In the present war, Germany could have pleaded that she was bound to take part by the terms of her alliance with Austria, who began it; but Britain would have been compelled to stand aloof. A very convenient arrangement for Germany, but not an arrangement that promised well for the peace of the world!

Even this rebuff did not dishearten Britain. Feeling that Germany might have some reasonable ground of complaint in the fact that her share of the extra-European world was so much less than that of France or of Britain herself, Britain attempted to come to an agreement on this head, such as would show that she had no desire to prevent the imperial expansion of Germany. A treaty was proposed and discussed, and was ready to be submitted to the proper authorities for confirmation in June 1914. It has never been made public, because the war cancelled it before it came into effect, and we do not know its terms. But we do know that the German colonial enthusiast, Paul Rohrbach, who has seen the draft treaty, has said that the concessions made by Britain were astonishingly extensive, and met every reasonable German demand. This sounds as if the proposals of the treaty, whatever they were, had been recklessly generous. But this much is clear, that the government which had this treaty in its possession when it forced on the war was not to be easily satisfied. It did not want merely external possessions. It wanted supremacy; it wanted world-dominion.

One last attempt the British government made in the frenzied days of negotiation which preceded the war. Sir Edward Grey had begged the German government to make ANY proposal which would make for peace, and promised his support beforehand; he had received no reply. He had undertaken that if Germany made any reasonable proposal, and France or Russia objected, he would have nothing further to do with France or Russia. Still there was no reply. Imagining that Germany might still be haunted by what Bismarck called 'the nightmare of coalition,' and might be rushing into war now because she feared a war in the future under more unfavourable conditions, he had pledged himself, if Germany would only say the word which would secure the peace, to use every effort to bring about a general understanding among the great powers which would banish all fears of an anti-German combination. It was of no use. The reply was the suggestion that Britain should bind herself to neutrality in this war on the following conditions: (a) that Germany should be given a free hand to violate the neutrality of Belgium (which Britain was bound by treaty to defend), on the understanding that Belgium should be reinstated after she had served her purpose, if she had offered no resistance; Belgium, be it noted, being bound in honour to offer resistance by the very treaty which Germany proposed to violate; and (b) that after France had been humiliated and beaten to the earth for the crime of possessing territories which Germany coveted, she should be restored to independence, and Germany should be content to annex her 5,000,000 square miles of colonies. In return for this undertaking Britain was to be — allowed to hold aloof from the war, and await her turn.

There is no getting over these facts. The aim of Germany had come to be nothing less than world-supremacy. The destiny of the whole globe was to be put to the test. Surely this was the very insanity of megalomania.

X
WHAT OF THE NIGHT?

The gigantic conflict into which the ambitions of Germany have plunged the world is the most tremendous event in human history, not merely because of the vast forces engaged, and the appalling volume of suffering which has resulted from it, but still more because of the magnitude of the principles for which it is being fought. It is a war to secure the right of communities which are linked together by the national spirit to determine their own destinies; it is a war to maintain the principles of humanity, the sanctity of formal undertakings between states, and the possibility of the co-operation of free peoples in the creation of a new and better world-order; it is a war between two principles of government, the principle of military autocracy and the principle of self-government. With all these aspects of the mighty struggle we are not here immediately concerned, though they have an intimate bearing upon our main theme: some of them have been analysed elsewhere.[9] But what does concern us most directly, and what makes this war the culmination of the long story which we have endeavoured to survey, is that this is a war in which, as in no earlier war, the whole fate and future of the now unified world is at stake. For just because the world is now, as never before, an indissoluble economic and political unity, the challenge of Germany, whatever view we may take of the immediate aims of the German state, inevitably raises the whole question of the principles upon which this unified world, unified by the victory of European civilisation, is to be in future directed. And the whole world knows, if vaguely, that these vast issues are at stake, and that this is no merely European conflict. That is why we see arrayed upon the fields of battle not only French, British, Russian, Italian, Serbian, Belgian, Rumanian, Greek and Portuguese soldiers, but Canadians, Australians, New Zealanders, South Africans, Indians, Algerians, Senegalese, Cambodians; and now, alongside of all these, the citizens of the American Republic. That is why Brazil and other states are hovering on the edge of the fray; why Japanese ships are helping to patrol the Mediterranean, why Arab armies are driving the Turk from the holy places of Mahomedanism, why African tribesmen are enrolled in new levies to clear the enemy out of his footholds in that continent. Almost the whole world is arrayed against the outlaw-power and her vassals. And the ultimate reason for this is that the whole world is concerned to see this terrible debate rightly determined.

[9] In Nationalism and Internationalism and in National Self-Government.

For the issue is as simple as this. Now that the world has been made one by the victory of Western civilisation, in what spirit is that supremacy to be used? Is it to be in the spirit expressed in the German Doctrine of Power, the spirit of mere dominion, ruthlessly imposed and ruthlessly exploited for the sole advantage of the master-power? That way ruin lies. Or is it to be in the spirit which has on the whole, and in spite of lapses, guided the progress of Western civilisation in the past, the spirit of respect for law and for the rights of the weak, the spirit of liberty which rejoices in variety of type and method, and which believes that the destiny towards which all peoples should be guided is that of self-government in freedom, and the co-operation of free peoples in the maintenance of common interests? Britain, France, and America have been the great advocates and exponents of these principles in the government of their own states: they are all ranged on one side to-day. Britain, also, as we have tried to show, has been led by Fate to take a chief part in the extension of these principles of Western civilisation to the non-European regions of the world; and, after many mistakes and failures, has in the direction of her own wide dominions found her way to a system which reconciles freedom with unity, and learned to regard herself as being only the trustee of civilisation in the government of the backward peoples whom she rules. For the just and final determination of such gigantic issues not even the terrible price we are paying is too high.

The issue of the great conflict lies still upon the lap of the gods. Yet one thing is, we may hope, already assured. Although at the beginning of the war they came near to winning it, the Germans are not now likely to win that complete victory upon which they had calculated, and which would have brought as its prize the mastery of the world. We can now form some judgment of the extent of the calamity which this would have meant for humanity. There would have remained in the world no power capable of resisting this grim and ugly tyrant-state, with its brute strength and bestial cruelty as of a gorilla in the primaeval forest, reinforced by the cold and pitiless calculus of the man of science in his laboratory; unless, perhaps, Russia had in time recovered her strength, or unless America had not merely thrown over her tradition of aloofness and made up her mind to intervene, but had been allowed the time to organise her forces for resistance. Of the great empires which the modern age has brought into being, the Russian would have survived as a helpless and blinded mammoth; the French Empire would have vanished, and the proud and noble land of France would have sunk into vassalage and despair; the British Empire would assuredly have dissolved into its component parts, for its strength is still too much concentrated in the motherland for it to be able to hold together once her power was broken. After a few generations, that will no longer be the case; but to-day it is so, and the dream of a partnership of free nations which had begun to dawn upon us would have been shattered for ever by a complete German victory. Some of the atoms of what once was an empire might have been left in freedom, but they would have been powerless to resist the decrees of the Master-state. There would have been one supreme world-power; and that a power whose attitude towards backward races has been illustrated by the ruthless massacre of the Hereros; whose attitude towards ancient but disorganised civilisations has been illustrated by the history of Kiao-chau and by the celebrated allocution of the Kaiser to his soldiers on the eve of the Boxer expedition, when he bade them outdo the ferocity of Attila and his Huns; whose attitude towards kindred civilisations on the same level as their own has been illustrated before the war in the treatment of Danes, Poles, and Alsatians, and during the war in the treatment of Belgium, of the occupied districts in France, of Poland and of Serbia. The world would have lain at the mercy of an insolent and ruthless tyranny, the tyranny of a Kultur whose ideal is the uniformity of a perfect mechanism, not the variety of life. Such a fate humanity could not long have tolerated; yet before the iron mechanism could have been shattered, if once it had been established, there must have been inconceivable suffering, and civilisation must have fallen back many stages towards barbarism. From this fate, we may perhaps claim, the world was saved from the moment when not Britain only, but the British Empire, refused to await its turn according to the German plan, threw its whole weight into the scale, and showed that, though not organised for war, it was not the effete and decadent power, not the fortuitous combination of discordant and incoherent elements, which German theory had supposed; but that Freedom can create a unity and a virile strength capable of withstanding even the most rigid discipline, capable of enduring defeat and disappointment undismayed; but incapable of yielding to the insolence of brute force.

It is still possible that the war may end in what is called an inconclusive peace; and as it is certain that of all her unrighteous gains that to which Germany will most desperately cling will be her domination over the Austrian and Turkish Empires, with the prospect which it affords of a later and more fortunate attempt at world-power, an inconclusive peace would mean that the whole world would live in constant dread of a renewal of these agonies and horrors in a still more awful form. What the effect of this would be upon the extra-European dominions of powers which would be drained of their manhood and loaded with the burden of the past war and the burden of preparation for the coming war, it is beyond our power to imagine. But it seems likely that the outer world would very swiftly begin to revise its judgment as to the value of that civilisation which it has, upon the whole, been ready to welcome; and chaos would soon come again.

Finally, it is possible that the Evil Power may be utterly routed, and the allied empires, tried by fire, may be given the opportunity and the obligation of making, not merely a new Europe, but a new world. If that chance should come, how will they use it? One thing at least is clear. The task which will face the diplomats who take part in the coming peace-congress will be different in kind as well as in degree from that of any of their predecessors at any moment in human history. They will be concerned not merely with the adjustment of the differences of a few leading states, and not merely with the settlement of Europe: they will have to deal with the whole world, and to decide upon what principles and to what ends the leadership of the peoples of European stock over the non-European world is to be exercised. Whether they realise it or not, whether they intend it or not, they will create either a world-order or a world-disorder. And it will inevitably be a world-disorder which will result unless we do some hard thinking on this gigantic problem which faces us, and unless we are prepared to learn, from the history of the relations of Europe with the outer world, what are the principles by which we ought to be guided. We are too prone, when we think of the problems of the future peace, to fix our attention almost wholly upon Europe, and, if we think of the non-European world at all, to assume either that the problem is merely one of power, or that the principles which will guide us in the settlement of Europe can be equally applied outside of Europe. Both of these assumptions are dangerous, because both disregard the teachings of the past which we have been surveying.

If, on the one hand, we are content to regard the problem as merely one of power, and to divide out the non-European world among the victors as the spoils of victory, we shall indeed have been conquered by the very spirit which we are fighting; we shall have become converts to the German Doctrine of Power, which has brought upon us all these ills, and may bring yet more appalling evils in the future. The world will emerge divided among a group of vast empires which will overshadow the lesser states. These empires will continue to regard one another with fear and suspicion, and to look upon their subject-peoples merely as providing the implements for a war of destruction, to be waged by cut-throat commercial rivalry in time of peace, and by man-power and machine-power in war. If that should be the result of all our agonies, the burden which must be laid upon the peoples of these empires, and the intolerable anticipation of what is to come, will make their yoke seem indeed a heavy one; will probably bring about their disintegration;

and will end that ascendancy of Western civilisation over the world which the last four centuries have established. And justly; since Western civilisation will thus be made to stand not for justice and liberty, but for injustice and oppression. Such must be the inevitable result of any settlement of the non-European world which is guided merely by the ambitions of a few rival states and the Doctrine of Power.

On the other hand, we are urged by enthusiasts for liberty, especially in Russia, to believe that imperialism as such is the enemy; that we must put an end for ever to all dominion exercised by one people over another; and that outside of Europe as within it we must trust to the same principles for the hope of future peace—the principles of national freedom and self-government—and leave all peoples everywhere to control freely their own destinies. But this is a misreading of the facts as fatal as the other. It disregards the value of the work that has been done in the extension of European civilisation to the rest of the world by the imperial activities of the European peoples. It fails to recognise that until Europe began to conquer the world neither rational law nor political liberty had ever in any real sense existed in the outer world, and that their dominion is even now far from assured, but depends for its maintenance upon the continued tutelage of the European peoples. It fails to realise that the economic demands of the modern world necessitate the maintenance of civilised administration after the Western pattern, and that this can only be assured, in large regions of the earth, by means of the political control of European peoples. Above all this view does not grasp the essential fact that the idea of nationhood and the idea of self-government are both modern ideas, which have had their origin in Europe, and which can only be realised among peoples of a high political development; that the sense of nationhood is but slowly created, and must not be arbitrarily defined in terms of race or language; and that the capacity for self-government is only formed by a long process of training, and has never existed except among peoples who were unified by a strongly felt community of sentiment, and had acquired the habit and instinct of loyalty to the law. Assuredly it is the duty of Europe and America to extend these fruitful conceptions to the regions which have passed under their influence. But the process must be a very slow one, and it can only be achieved under tutelage. It is the control of the European peoples over the non-European world which has turned the world into an economic unit, brought it within a single political system, and opened to us the possibility of making a world-order such as the most daring dreamers of the past could never have conceived. This control cannot be suddenly withdrawn. For a very long time to come the world-states whose rise we have traced must continue to be the means by which the political discoveries of Europe, as well as her material civilisation, are made available for the rest of the world. The world-states are such recent things that we have not yet found a place for them in our political philosophy. But unless we find a place for them, and think in terms of them, in the future, we shall be in danger of a terrible shipwreck.

If, then, it is essential, not only for the economic development of the world, but for the political advancement of its more backward peoples, that the political suzerainty of the European peoples should survive, and as a consequence that the world should continue to be dominated by a group of great world-states, how are we to conjure away the nightmare of inter-imperial rivalry which has brought upon us the present catastrophe, and seems to threaten us with yet more appalling ruin in the future? Only by resolving and ensuring, as at the great settlement we may be able to do, that the necessary political control of Europe over the outer world shall in future be exercised not merely in the interests of the mistress-states, but in accordance with principles which are just in themselves, and which will give to all peoples a fair chance of making the best use of their powers. But how are we to discover these principles, if the ideas of nationality and self-government, to which we pin our faith in Europe, are to be held inapplicable to the greater part of the non-European world? There is only one possible source of instruction: our past experience, which has now extended over four centuries, and which we have in this book endeavoured to survey.

Now while it is undeniably true that the mere lust of power has always been present in the imperial activities of the European peoples, it is certainly untrue (as our study ought to have shown) that it has ever been the sole motive, except, perhaps, in the great German challenge. And in the course of their experience the colonising peoples have gradually worked out certain principles in their treatment of subject peoples, which ought to be of use to us. The fullest and the most varied experience is that of the British Empire: it is the oldest of all the world-states; it alone includes regions of the utmost variety of types, new lands peopled by European settlers, realms of ancient civilisation like India, and regions inhabited by backward and primitive peoples. It would be absurd to claim that its methods are perfect and infallible. But they have been very varied, and quite astonishingly successful. And it is because they seem to afford clearer guidance than any other part of the experiments which we have recorded that we have studied them, especially in their later developments, with what may have seemed a disproportionate fulness. What are the principles which experience has gradually worked out in the British Empire? They cannot be embodied in a single formula, because they vary according to the condition and development of the lands to which they apply.

But in the first place we have learnt by a very long experience that in lands inhabited by European settlers, who bring with them European traditions, the only satisfactory solution is to be found in the concession of the fullest self-governing rights, since these settlers are able to use them, and in the encouragement of that sentiment of unity which we call the national spirit. And this involves a recognition of the fact that nationality is never to be defined solely in terms of race or language, but can arise, and should be encouraged to arise, among racially divided communities such as Canada and South Africa. Any attempt to interpret nationhood in terms of race is not merely dangerous, but ruinous; and such endeavours to stimulate or accentuate racial conflict, as Germany has been guilty of in Brazil, in South Africa, and even in America, must be, if successful, fatal to the progress of the countries affected, and dangerous to the peace of the world.

In the second place we have learnt that in lands of ancient civilisation, where ruling castes have for centuries been in the habit of exploiting their subjects, the supreme gift which Europe can offer is that of internal peace and a firmly administered and equal law, which will render possible the gradual rise of a sense of unity, and the gradual training of the people in the habits of life that make self-government possible. How soon national unity can be established, or self-government made practicable in any full sense, must be matter of debate. But the creation of these things is, or ought to be, the ultimate aim of European government in such countries. And in the meantime, and until they become fully masters of their own fate, these lands, so our British experience tells us, ought to be treated as distinct political units; they should pay no tribute; all their resources should be devoted to their own development; and they should not be expected or required to maintain larger forces than are necessary for their own defence. At the same time, the ruling power should claim no special privileges for its own citizens, but should throw open the markets of such realms equally to all nations. In short it should act not as a master, but as a trustee, on behalf of its subjects and also on behalf of civilisation.

In the third place we have learnt that in the backward regions of the earth it is the duty of the ruling power, firstly, to protect its primitive subjects from unscrupulous exploitation, to guard their simple customs, proscribing only those which are immoral, and to afford them the means of a gradual emancipation from barbarism; secondly, to develop the economic resources of these regions for the needs of the industrial world, to open them up by modern communications, and to make them available on equal terms to all nations, giving no advantage to its own citizens.

In spite of lapses and defects, it is an undeniable historical fact that these are the principles which have been wrought out and applied in the administration of the British Empire during the nineteenth century. They are not vague and Utopian dreams; they are a matter of daily practice. If they can be applied by one of the world-states, and that the greatest, why should they not be applied by the rest? But if these principles became universal, is it not apparent that all danger of a catastrophic war between these powers would be removed, since every reason for it would have vanished? Thus the necessary and advantageous tutelage of Europe over the non-European world, and the continuance of the great world-states, could be combined with the conjuring away of the ever-present terror of war, and with the gradual training of the non-European peoples to enjoy the political methods of Europe; while the lesser states without extra-European dominions need no longer feel themselves stunted and reduced to economic dependence upon their great neighbours. Thus, and thus alone, can the benefits of the long development which we have traced be reaped in full; thus alone can the dominion of the European peoples over the world be made to mean justice and the chance for all peoples to make the best of their powers.

But it is not only the principles upon which particular areas outside of Europe should be governed which we must consider. We must reflect also upon the nature of the relations that should exist between the various members of these great world-empires, which must hence-forward be the dominating factors in the world's politics. And here the problem is urgent only in the case of the British Empire, because it alone is developed to such a point that the problem is inevitably raised. Whatever else may happen, the war must necessarily bring a crisis in the history of the British Empire. On a vastly greater scale the situation of 1763 is being reproduced. Now, as then, the Empire will emerge from a war for existence, in which mother and daughter lands alike have shared. Now, as then, the strain and pressure of the war will have brought to light deficiencies in the system of the Empire. Now, as then, the most patent of these deficiencies will be the fact that, generous as the self-governing powers of the great Dominions have been, they still have limits; and the irresistible tendency of self-government to work towards its own fulfilment will once more show itself. For there are two spheres in which even the most fully self-governing of the empire-nations have no effective control: they do not share in the determination of foreign policy, and they do not share in the direction of imperial defence. The responsibility for foreign policy, and the responsibility, and with it almost the whole burden, of organising imperial defence, have hitherto rested solely with Britain. Until the Great War, foreign policy seemed to be a matter of purely European interest, not directly concerning the great Dominions; nor did the problems of imperial defence appear very pressing or urgent. But now all have realised that not merely their interests, but their very existence, may depend upon the wise conduct of foreign relations; and now all have contributed the whole available strength of their manhood to support a struggle in whose direction they have had no effective share. These things must henceforth be altered; and they can be altered only in one or other of three ways. Either the great Dominions will become independent states, as the American colonies did, and pursue a foreign policy and maintain a system of defence of their own; or the Empire must reshape itself as a sort of permanent offensive and defensive alliance, whose external policy and modes of defence will be arranged by agreement; or some mode of common management of these and other questions must be devised. The first of these solutions is unlikely to be adopted, not only because the component members of the Empire are conscious of their individual weakness, but still more because the memory of the ordeal through which all have passed must form an indissoluble bond. Yet rashness or high-handedness in the treatment of the great issue might lead even to this unlikely result. If either of the other two solutions is adopted, the question will at once arise of the place to be occupied, in the league or in the reorganised super-state, of all those innumerable sections of the Empire which do not yet enjoy, and some of which may never enjoy, the full privileges of self-government; and above all, the place to be taken by the vast dominion of India, which though it is not, and may not for a long time become, a fully self-governing state, is yet a definite and vitally important unit in the Empire, entitled to have its needs and problems considered, and its government represented, on equal terms with the rest. The problem is an extraordinarily difficult one; perhaps the most difficult political problem that has ever faced the sons of men. But it is essentially the same problem which has continually recurred in the history of British imperialism, though it now presents itself on a vastly greater scale, and in a far more complex form, than ever before: it is the problem of reconciling unity with liberty and variety; of combining nationality and self-government with imperialism, without impairing the rights of either. And beyond any doubt the most tremendous and fascinating political question which now awaits solution in the world, is the question whether the political instinct of the British peoples, and the genius of self-government, will find a way out of these difficulties, as they have found a way out of so many others. Patience, mutual tolerance, willingness to compromise, will be required in the highest measure if the solution is to be found; but these are the qualities which self-government cultivates.

'A thing that is wholly a sham,' said Treitschke, speaking of the British Empire, 'cannot in this world of ours, endure for ever.' Why did this Empire appear to Treitschke to be 'wholly a sham'? Was it not because it did not answer to any definition of the word 'Empire' to be found in German political philosophy; because it did not mean dominion and uniformity, but liberty and variety; because it did not rest upon Force, as, in his view, every firmly established state must do; because it was not governed by a single master, whose edicts all its subjects must obey? But for 'a thing that is wholly a sham' men do not lay down their lives, in thousands and in hundreds of thousands, not under the pressure of compulsion, but by a willing self-devotion; for the defence of 'a thing that is wholly a sham' men will not stream in from all the ends of the earth, abandoning their families and their careers, and offering without murmur or hesitation themselves and all they have and are. There must be a reality in the thing that calls forth such sacrifices, a reality of the kind to which Realpolitik, with its concentration upon purely material concerns, is wholly blind: it is the reality of an ideal of honour, and justice, and freedom. And if the Germans have been deceived in their calculations of Realpolitik, is it not perhaps because they have learnt to regard honour, and justice, and freedom as 'things that are wholly shams'?

This amazing political structure, which refuses to fall within any of the categories of political science, which is an empire and yet not an empire, a state and yet not a state, a super-nation incorporating in itself an incredible variety of peoples and races, is not a structure which has been designed by the ingenuity of man, or created by the purposive action of a government; it is a natural growth, the product of the spontaneous activity of innumerable individuals and groups springing from among peoples whose history has made liberty and the tolerance of differences their most fundamental instincts; it is the outcome of a series of accidents, unforeseen, but turned to advantage by the unfailing and ever-new resourcefulness of men habituated to self-government. There is no logic or uniformity in its system, which has arisen from an infinite number of makeshifts and tentative experiments, yet in all of these a certain consistency appears, because they have been presided over by the genius of self-government. It is distributed over every continent, is washed by every ocean, includes half the dust of islands that Nature has scattered about the seas of the world, controls almost all the main avenues of the world's sea-going commerce, and is linked together by ten thousand ships perpetually going to and fro. Weak for offensive purposes, because its resources are so scattered, it is, except at a few points, almost impregnable against attack, if its forces are well organised. It includes among its population representatives of almost every human race and religion, and every grade of civilisation, from the Australian Bushman to the subtle and philosophic Brahmin, from the African dwarf to the master of modern industry or the scholar of universities. Almost every form of social organisation and of government known to man is represented in its complex and many-hued fabric. It embodies five of the most completely self-governing communities which the world has known, and four of these control the future of the great empty spaces that remain for the settlement of white men. It finds place for the highly organised caste system by which the teeming millions of India are held together. It preserves the simple tribal organisation of the African clans. To different elements among its subjects this empire appears in different aspects. To the self-governing Dominions it is a brotherhood of free nations, co-operating for the defence and diffusion of common ideas and of common institutions. To the ancient civilisations of India or of Egypt it is a power which, in spite of all its mistakes and limitations, has brought peace instead of turmoil, law instead of arbitrary might, unity instead of chaos, justice instead of oppression, freedom for the development of the capacities and characteristic ideas of their peoples, and the prospect of a steady growth of national unity and political responsibility. To the backward races it has meant the suppression of unending slaughter, the disappearance of slavery, the protection of the rights and usages of primitive and simple folk against reckless exploitation, and the chance of gradual improvement and emancipation from barbarism. But to all alike, to one quarter of the inhabitants of the world, it has meant the establishment of the Reign of Law, and of the Liberty which can only exist under its shelter. In some degree, though imperfectly as yet, it has realised within its own body all the three great political ideas of the modern world. It has fostered the rise of a sense of nationhood in the young communities of the new lands, and in the old and decaying civilisations of the most ancient historic countries. It has given a freedom of development to self-government such as history has never before known. And by linking together so many diverse and contrasted peoples in a common peace, it has already realised, for a quarter of the globe, the ideal of internationalism on a scale undreamt of by the most sanguine prophets of Europe.

Truly this empire is a fabric so wonderful, so many-sided, and so various in its aspects, that it may well escape the rigid categories of a German professor, and seem to him 'wholly a sham.' Now is the crisis of its fate: and if the wisdom of its leaders can solve the riddle of the Sphinx which is being put to them, the Great War will indeed have brought, for a quarter of the world, the culmination of modern history.